The
CHEMICAL ELEMENTS
David E. Newton

A Venture Book

FRANKLIN WATTS
New York ■ Chicago ■ London ■ Toronto ■ Sydney

To Phyllis Cowlishaw

How much better the world would be
If all neighbors were like Phyllis!

3 9082 05021513 9

Photographs copyright ©: Photo Researchers, Inc.: pp. 1 (J. L. Charmet/SPL), 4,
10 bottom, 11 top, 12, 13 (all Lawrence Migdale/Science Source), 6 top,
10 top (both Rich Treptow), 6 bottom (Department of Energy), 8 top (Harold
Hoffman), 8 bottom (Bruce Roberts), 9 top (M. Claye/Jacana), 9 bottom (F. B.
Grunzweig), 11 bottom (Ken Eward/SS), 13 bottom (Will McIntyre), 14 (Bjorn
Bolstad), 15 top (Dale E. Boyer), 15 bottom (Lynn McLaren), 16 (C. J. Collins);
Fundamental Photos Inc./Richard Megna: pp. 5, 7.

Library of Congress Cataloging-in-Publication Data

Newton, David E.
The chemical elements / by David E. Newton.
p.   cm.—(A Venture book)
Includes bibliographical references and index.
ISBN 0-531-12501-7
1. Chemical elements—Juvenile literature.   [1. Chemical elements.]
I. Title.
QD466.N46   1994
93-30044 CIP AC
546—dc20

OCT 1 7 1994

Copyright © 1994 by Instructional Horizons, Inc.
All rights reserved
Printed in the United States of America
6 5 4 3 2 1

Contents

Prologue

A metal soft enough to be cut with a knife. Another that will melt in the heat of your hand. A waxy solid that glows in the dark. A gas so reactive that it explodes if it comes into contact with water.

Welcome to the wonderful world of the chemical elements! Everything in nature is made up of about 100 basic materials called elements. These substances have a wide variety of interesting properties. Humans have found an almost unlimited number of ways to use these properties in applications that range from airplane bodies to insecticides to life-support systems.

Our purpose is to help you learn more about the chemical elements: how they were discovered, where they occur in nature, what some of their properties are, and how they are used by humans. Of course, we can't go into a lot of detail about any one element or its applications. There is hardly enough space to do more than introduce you to each of the 100-odd elements. But perhaps you will find out enough to want to learn more about one or more of these fascinating substances.

1

What Is an Element?

What is the natural world made of? At first glance, nature appears to consist of countless numbers of very different materials: oak, pine, and maple wood; sandstone, limestone, and marble; emerald, diamond, and sapphire; lead, tin, and iron; hair, teeth, and bone; and so on. The world appears to be an extremely complex mixture of many different materials.

But philosophers and scientists have long held another view of the world. They have found it difficult to believe that nature is *really* as complex as it appears to be. Instead, they have assumed that the many different materials we see result from the combination of a small number of fundamental substances called *elements*. The term *element* refers to a basic substance that cannot be broken down into anything simpler by ordinary chemical or physical means. Thus, gold is considered to be an element because, no matter what you do to it, you cannot reduce it to anything simpler than itself.

EARLY CONCEPTS OF THE ELEMENTS

The idea of an element probably originated with the ancient Greeks. At first, philosophers imagined that only one basic substance exists. They believed that everything was made of some variation of that substance. For example, Thales (624– 546 B.C.) taught that everything is made from water. By condensing, evaporating, and changing its outward form, water could take the appearance of all other materials, he said. Anaximenes (about 570–500 B.C.) held a similar view, but called air the one single element. For Heraclitus (about 540–475 B.C.), fire was the elementary material from which everything else was formed.

Other philosophers claimed that two or more elements were necessary. Probably the most popular view was that of Aristotle (384–322 B.C.), who taught that earth, air, fire, and water were the four elementary materials. Aristotle's ideas were quite different from modern concepts of an element. He thought that certain "qualities" were elemental. For example, when he talked about "earth" as an element, he meant a certain quality of "heaviness," not the dirt in your back yard. Thus, a piece of paper might be thought of as consisting of some "earth" (because it was somewhat heavy), some "water" (because it is "bendable," or "fluid," like water), and a little "air" (because it is lighter than other types of earth).

Other scholars proposed other theories of the elements. Works credited to the Arabian philosopher Jabir ibn Hayyan (eighth or ninth century A.D.), for example, described only two elements, mercury and sulfur. European philosophers of the Middle Ages sometimes added a third substance, salt, to this list.

MODERN CONCEPTS OF AN ELEMENT

As modern chemistry began to develop, questions about the nature of an element became more confused. Some scholars tried to keep the Greek concept of a handful of fundamental substances that might or might not be material substances. Others were aware of the increasing number of new materials being discovered that seemed to be "fundamental" materials.

In 1661, the English philosopher Robert Boyle tried to resolve this issue. In his book, *Sceptical Chymist*, Boyle rejected the Greek idea of elements as being nonmaterial "qualities." Instead, he suggested that the term *element* be reserved for "certain Primitive and Simple, or perfectly unmingled bodies; which not being made up of any other bodies, or of one another, are the Ingredients of which all those call'd perfectly mixt Bodies are immediately compounded, and into which they are ultimately resolved."

Boyle's concept of an element differs from that of a modern chemist. But it is important because it helped scholars to start seeing the elements in a different light, namely as concrete materials and not "qualities."

The next step in understanding the nature of elements was provided by Antoine-Laurent Lavoisier (1743–94), often called the Father of Modern Chemistry. In his 1789 textbook on chemistry, *Traité Elémentaire de Chimie*, Lavoisier wrote that "all substances which we have not yet been able by any means to decompose are elements to us."

The definition that Lavoisier provided in 1789 is still considered valid today even though the specific list of elements that accompanied that definition has changed. For example, Lavoisier was correct in listing gold, silver, mercury, and sulfur among the elements. But he was not correct in including caloric (heat) and lumière (light).

In fact, the search for substances that are true elements occupied scientists for more than 100 years after Lavoisier's time. At least 100 "false elements" were uncovered in addition to nearly as many true elements. The problem was that, until Moseley's discovery of atomic number in 1913, scientists had no way of knowing how many elements could exist. There was no reason to know that there might be 50, or 100, or 200. Moseley was able to show, however, that scientists could never expect to discover more than about 100 elements.

THE ELEMENTS TODAY

Scientists now know that they have discovered all the elements—ninety-two of them—that exist in the natural world. In addition, they have found ways to produce another dozen or so synthetic elements. Some of these elements may have existed on the earth millions or billions of years ago, but they can no longer be detected in the natural world.

The 100-odd chemical elements have a wide variety of chemical and physical properties. The vast majority are metal-like substances: hard, solid, lustrous, capable of being hammered into thin sheets or drawn into fine wires. Iron, tin, nickel, magnesium, and aluminum are familiar examples of these metallic elements.

A few of the metallic elements have special properties that set them off from their cousins. In some cases it is color (gold and copper, for example) or physical state. Mercury, for example, is a liquid and gallium melts at body temperature. The three heaviest metals give off radiation, changing spontaneously into new elements.

The nonmetallic elements exist in even greater variety. Eleven are gases. Hydrogen, helium, oxygen, and nitrogen are examples. One—bromine—is a liquid. Others are solids with many different colors, textures, and *crystalline* forms. Sulfur can be a yellow powder or a dark-red plastic; phosphorus can exist in at least five forms, including a waxy white solid, a red powder, and black crystals. Iodine occurs as a steel-gray solid, but through *sublimation* forms a beautiful violet vapor. A few substances—the metalloids or semimetals—can look and behave as metals or nonmetals. Silicon, arsenic, and antimony are among these elements.

As chemists discovered more and more elements with a great variety of properties, a gnawing question began to emerge. Are the chemical elements really as different as they seem? Or is there some underlying principle that can be used to organize the apparent complexity that exists?

2

Organizing the Elements

By the mid-nineteenth century, chemists had discovered more than sixty elements. New elements were being announced every few years. Two questions began to trouble scientists. First, how many true elements were there? Was it correct to think that only a handful of these basic materials really existed? Or would chemists continue to find an unlimited number with passing time?

Second, was there some way that all these elements could be organized? Were there families or groups into which they could be arranged? Or were they all too different from each other to be classified in any way?

THE PERIODIC LAW

The answer to the second question was provided in 1869 almost simultaneously by two chemists, Dmitri Mendeleev in Russia and Lothar Meyer in Germany. Mendeleev and Meyer found a way to arrange the elements so that their properties were related to each other in a logical, orderly, and predictable way. This system of organization became known as the *periodic law.*

As with most discoveries in science, the periodic law did not appear "out of the blue." A number of scientists as far back as 1829 had foreseen some part of the periodic law. For example, in 1862, a French professor of geology, Alexandre

E. Beguyer de Chancourtois, invented the "telluric screw." He arranged the chemical elements according to their weights on a helical band that ran along the surface of a vertical cylinder. In this arrangement, elements with similar chemical and physical properties occurred above and below each other on the cylinder.

The efforts of Beguyer de Chancourtois and others were largely ignored by other scientists who could not see their significance or, worse, rejected them as "silly gimmicks."

That fate was not shared by the work of Meyer and Mendeleev. Both attacked the problem of organizing the elements in a similar way. They listed the elements according to their atomic weights, beginning with the lightest element, hydrogen. The *atomic weight* of an element is the total weight of all protons, neutrons, and electrons found in an atom of that element.

The following series shows what the first part of such a list looks like. The list makes use of the elements' chemical *symbols*, the "shorthand designation" by which they are often represented (for the elements' names, see periodic table in photo insert). The number below the symbol is the element's atomic weight (as of 1869).

H	Li	Be	B	C	N	O	F	Na	Mg	Al	Si	P
1	7	9	11	12	14	16	19	23	24	27	28	31

S	Cl	K	Ca
32	35.5	39	40

When the elements were arranged in this way, Mendeleev and Meyer found that a pattern began to emerge. Sodium (Na) is chemically similar to lithium (Li), magnesium (Mg) has properties like those of beryllium (Be), aluminum (Al) has properties similar to those of boron (B), and so on.

To illustrate this point, they rewrote the series, putting elements beneath those similar to them. The new list began to look like this:

H	Li	Be	B	C	N	O	F
1	7	9	11	12	14	16	19

	Na	Mg	Al	Si	P	S	Cl
	23	24	27	28	31	31	35.5

	K	Ca
	39	40

Notice that the elements are still in order, left to right and top to bottom. But they also fit together in such a way that similar elements (Li, Na, and K; Be, Mg, and Ca; B and Al, etc.) are together in a vertical column.

The Mendeleev-Meyer discovery is summarized in the *periodic law:* When the elements are arranged in order according to their atomic weights, their properties are repeated in a periodic way. The term *periodic* means that something is repeated on a regular basis. The ebb and flow of the tides is an example of a periodic pattern.

Credit for the discovery of the periodic law is usually given primarily to Mendeleev for two reasons. First, he used a more complete set of data in working out his version of the law. Second, and more important, he showed how the law could be used to predict the existence of new elements.

PREDICTIONS AND PROBLEMS

Mendeleev was able to predict the existence of new elements because of gaps that appeared in his original table of the elements. Reproduced next is a portion of that original table.

Notice that the next heavier element after calcium (Ca) in the chart is titanium (Ti). Normally, one would expect to see Ti immediately after Ca, below aluminum (Al).

Na	Mg	Al	Si	P
23	24	27	28	31

K	Ca		Ti	V
39	40		48	51

But Mendeleev knew that would be a mistake. In his table, like elements always occurred below each other, and titanium is like silicon (Si), not aluminum. So Mendeleev put titanium where it belonged on the basis of its properties. Then he predicted that a new element would be found to fill the missing space beneath aluminum. In 1879, the Swedish chemist L. F. Nilson discovered the missing element and named it *scandium.*

Mendeleev's periodic law was quickly accepted by most chemists. However, it still contained a few problems. Look at the modern version of the periodic table in the photo insert. Notice that tellurium (Te) and iodine (I) appear to be in the wrong order: tellurium has an atomic weight greater than iodine's and should, therefore, *follow* it. Mendeleev guessed that chemists had made an error in calculating the weight of either tellurium or iodine.

But this time, Mendeleev was wrong. The correct explanation for this apparent confusion did not appear for nearly 50 years. Then the English physicist H. G. J. Moseley unraveled the puzzle. Moseley found that the elements can also be arranged according to their *atomic number* (the number of protons in their nuclei). This arrangement is almost—but not exactly—the same as the atomic weight sequence.

However, when atomic numbers are used instead of

atomic weights in building the periodic table, all problems remaining from Mendeleev's original work disappear. The result is the table shown in the photo insert. In this table, the decimal number in each square is the element's atomic weight and the whole number, its atomic number.

ATOMIC STRUCTURE AND PERIODIC PROPERTIES

Meyer, Mendeleev, and Moseley had no way of knowing *why* the periodic law is true. The statements they wrote simply described patterns that they observed among the elements. But they did not know why these properties depended on atomic weight or atomic number.

Today, chemists understand the connection between an element's atomic number and its properties. Figure 1 is a simplified diagram of the sodium *atom*. The atom consists of 11 *protons* and 12 *neutrons* in its nucleus and 11 *electrons* arranged in three shells outside the nucleus. The first shell contains 2 electrons, the second shell 8 electrons, and the third shell 1 electron.

Chemists now know that an element's properties depend largely on the number of electrons in its outer shell. All atoms with one electron in their outer shell have similar properties. All atoms with two electrons in their outer shell also behave alike. And so on.

But the number of electrons in an atom is always the same as the number of protons in the atom's *nucleus*. Each proton carries a charge of $+1$, and each electron carries a charge of -1. Since all atoms are electrically neutral, the number of protons must always be the same as the number of electrons.

Now recall that the number of protons in an atom is its atomic number. So it follows that an element's atomic number also reflects the number of electrons in one of its atoms. Therefore, the properties of an element (determined by the arrangement of electrons in its atoms) is closely related to its

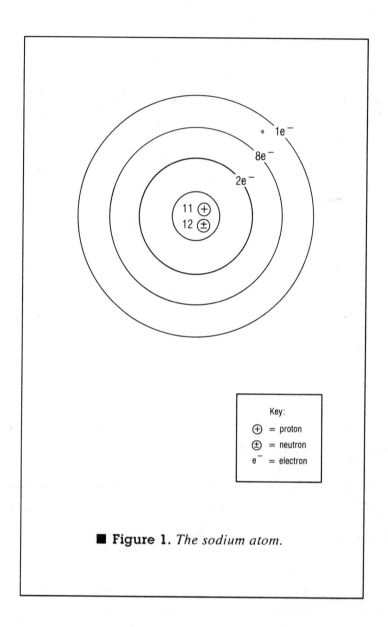

■ Figure 1. *The sodium atom.*

atomic number (the number of protons in the nucleus of its atoms). Thus, the periodic law!

Atomic weight is not as useful in establishing the periodic law. The atomic weight of an atom includes neutrons, which carry no electric charge. The fact that two atoms have different numbers of neutrons has no effect on the number of electrons they contain and, thus, on their properties. The match between atomic weight and properties is, therefore, close, but not exact.

PATTERNS IN THE PERIODIC TABLE

Chemists and students of science find the periodic table to be an invaluable tool. Imagine, for example, that the author of this book had to describe each element to you individually. If he spent only 2 or 3 pages on each element, the book would be nearly 300 pages long! Even then, you would not learn very much about each element.

But the periodic table allows another approach. The author can talk about groups of elements that have similar properties. He can spend more time describing what four, five, or more elements are like *at once*.

This approach is possible because of certain patterns in the periodic table. One pattern consists of the vertical columns of related elements known as *families* of elements. The families are sometimes called by names, as human families are. The elements in column 1, for example, are known as the *alkali metals*, while those in column 2 are the *alkaline earth metals*.

The members of a chemical family are similar to each other because they all have similar electronic structures. The atoms that make up all of the elements in column 1, for example, have one electron in their outermost shell. The atoms of elements in column 7 all have seven electrons in their outermost shell. And so on.

Sometimes, the families are referred to simply by the number at the top of their columns. The problem is that

European and American chemists have used two different systems for numbering columns. A decision was made in the 1980s to resolve this confusion and use the European system. But many American chemists disagree with that decision and continue to use the one they've always used. Thus, both systems of numbering are shown in the periodic table in the photo insert.

In the American system, the Roman numeral at the top of the column usually corresponds to the number of electrons in the outermost orbit of the atoms that make up the elements in this column. For example, the atoms that make up the elements in column IIIB all have 3 electrons in their outermost orbit. Elements in column VA are made of atoms that have 5 electrons in their outermost orbit. This general rule is not true in every instance, however.

The properties of the elements in any family change in an orderly way as you move down the periodic table. The following chart shows one such pattern for the members of the alkali family.

Element	Melting Point ° C	Boiling Point ° C	Density g/cm³
Li	180.5	1347	0.534
Na	97.8	881.4	0.968
K	63.2	765.5	0.856
Rb	39.0	688	1.532
Cs	28.5	705	1.90

You should be able to find two places in this chart where properties do not change in a completely orderly fashion. All that shows is that the periodic law shows general trends, but not absolutely perfect patterns.

Another pattern in the periodic table is represented in the horizontal arrangement, or *row*, of elements. In going from left to right along any one row, the properties of the elements in that row also tend to show regular changes. For example, look at the ionization energies of the elements in row 2. The *ionization energy* of an element is the energy needed to remove an electron from an atom of the element.

Element	Li	Be	B	C	N	O	F	Ne
Ionization Energy (in electron volts)	5.4	9.3	8.3	11.3	14.5	13.6	17.4	21.6

Again, these changes in properties correspond to changes in electronic structure. Compare the number of electrons in the outermost orbit of the atoms in each element of row 2, as shown next, with the ionization energies shown previously.

Element	Li	Be	B	C	N	O	F	Ne
Number of electrons in outermost orbit	1	2	3	4	5	6	7	8

You can see that as the number of electrons in the outermost shell of an atom increases, so does the ionization energy of that atom.

Notice how different the rows are in length. Row 1 contains only 2 elements, hydrogen (H) and helium (He). Rows 2 and 3 contain 8 elements each, and rows 4 and 5 contain 18 each. Rows 6 and 7 actually contain 32 elements each. These rows are so long that one section is removed from each row and printed at the bottom in order to fit the table on a standard sheet of paper. You can see where these sections have been removed by the asterisk (*) and dagger (†) in the main table.

The middle section of the periodic table, between columns 2 (IIA) and 13 (IIIB), is called the *transition elements*. Those that have been pulled out of row 6 are called the *lanthanides* and those taken from row 7, the *actinides*.

Finally, notice the diagonal line that runs down the right

side of the table. The elements to the left of that line are the *metals*, indicated by white boxes. Those to the right of the line are *nonmetals*, indicated by gray boxes. Those immediately on either side of the line are *metalloids* or *semimetals*, indicated by cross-hatched boxes.

This introduction to the periodic table can be of great help in learning about the chemical elements. This book may not tell you everything you want to know about cesium (Cs), for example. But you can locate Cs in the periodic table and see what family (column) and row it is in. Then, you can refer to the general information about that family and row to learn some general properties of cesium.

3:

The Alkali Metals

Some of the most interesting and unusual of the chemical elements appear in the alkali family. Lithium, sodium, potassium, rubidium, cesium, and francium are all metals, but some of their properties are not what one might expect of a metal. Sodium and potassium are soft enough to cut with a knife and have a density so low that they will float on water.

But you would normally not *want* to try floating them since they react vigorously with water. In that reaction, they give off hydrogen gas, which may be ignited by the heat of the metal-water reaction. What you see when you put potassium in water, for example, is a globule of molten potassium metal, fizzing and spitting around on the water's surface, popping and burning with a pretty violet flame.

The metal occurs as a globule because it—like the other alkali metals—has a very low melting point. Heat produced in the metal-water reaction is sufficient to melt the metal and change it into a liquid.

DISCOVERY OF THE ALKALI METALS

Sodium and potassium are among the most common elements on earth, ranking seventh and eighth, respectively, in the earth's crust. Yet, they were not isolated as pure elements until relatively late in chemical history. The reason is that most reactions used by chemists take place in water.

You have already found out what happens when an alkali metal comes into contact with water! For this reason attempts to isolate the alkali metals by conventional methods were unsuccessful.

The first preparation of an alkali metal required, therefore, the use of an entirely new technique. In 1807, the twenty-nine-year-old English chemist Humphry Davy passed an electrical current through molten (melted) potash, a common mineral of potassium. At one electrode in his apparatus, Davy observed tiny globules of molten potassium metal, the first time a pure alkali metal had been seen. A few days later, he repeated the experiment with molten caustic soda, a compound that contains sodium, and obtained pure sodium metal. Davy named potassium and sodium after the minerals from which they were obtained, potash and caustic soda.

Lithium was the next alkali metal to be discovered. In 1817, the Swedish chemist Johan August Arfvedson found the element in the minerals petalite and spodumene. He named the element after the Greek word *lithos*, for "stone."

Cesium and rubidium were discovered within a year of each other. The German chemists Robert Bunsen and Gustav Kirchoff had discovered in 1859 the principle of the spectroscope. The spectroscope is a device for viewing the flames produced when a substance is heated or burned. Lines observable in the spectroscope allow a chemist to identify the elements present in the substance being heated.

On May 10, 1860, Bunsen and Kirchoff announced that they had found signs of an entirely new element. They gave the name *cesium* to the element because of its blue (*caesius* = "blue color of the sky") spectral lines. Less than a year later, on February 23, 1861, they announced the discovery of a second new element. *Rubidium* was also named because of the color of its spectral lines (*rubidus* = "deepest red").

Francium was the last of the alkali metals to be discovered. The French chemist Marguerite Perey discovered the element in 1939 and named it after her homeland. Francium is one of the rarest and least understood of the elements. Chemists estimate that no more than 15 to 25 grams of the element occurs in all of the earth's crust.

OCCURRENCE OF THE ALKALI METALS

Sodium and potassium (like the other alkali metals) do not occur free in nature because they are much too active. Compounds of both elements are abundant, however. The world's oceans are an enormous reserve of both sodium chloride and potassium chloride. According to one estimate, the amount of both compounds in the earth's oceans is equivalent to a mass one and a half times that of the North American continent.

Sodium occurs widely in the earth's crust as rock salt (sodium chloride [$NaCl$]), sodium carbonate (Na_2CO_3), sodium nitrate (saltpeter [$NaNO_3$]), sodium sulfate (Na_2SO_4), and borax (sodium tetraborate [$Na_2B_4O_7$]). The most abundant of these, rock salt, is produced when salt water from oceans evaporates. Salt beds hundreds of meters thick—the remains of ancient seas—can be found in many parts of the world. Salt can be dug out from underground mines near Detroit, Michigan, for example, in much the same way that coal is removed from underground mines.

The process by which such salt beds are formed is still occurring in places such as the Great Salt Lake and the Dead Sea. The United States produces about a quarter of the world's rock salt, more than two and a half times as much as the second largest producer (China).

Potassium chloride (KCl) also occurs widely in the earth's oceans and in salt beds. But its abundance is only about 3 percent that of sodium chloride. About half of the world's potassium chloride comes from Russia and Canada, and the United States produces about 10 percent of the world's supply.

Lithium, rubidium, and cesium occur primarily in minerals in the earth's crust. Rubidium is the most abundant of the three (78 parts per million [ppm]), about four times as abundant as lithium (18 ppm) and 30 times as abundant as cesium (2.6 ppm). The three metals rank numbers 23, 35, and 45 in abundance in the earth's crust.

USES OF THE ALKALI METALS AND THEIR COMPOUNDS

The pure alkali metals have relatively few uses. For many years, sodium was used in the production of tetraethyl lead, an antiknocking agent added to gasoline. But the environmental hazards of lead compounds have led to a sharp decline in this application. A growing demand for the metal has taken place in the nuclear power industry, where liquid sodium is used as a heat-exchange medium in fast breeder nuclear reactors. The metal is also used in the production of titanium, zirconium, and some other metals.

In contrast to the pure metals, the alkali metal compounds have an enormous number of applications. Historically, the most important commercial compound of sodium has been sodium chloride, or rock salt. It is the starting point from which a host of other compounds are produced. In fact, the chemical industry may be said to have begun with one such process, the conversion of sodium chloride to sodium hydroxide (NaOH).

In 1787, Nicolas Leblanc, physician to the Duke of Orleans, invented a method for converting the abundant compound rock salt to the valuable but less common compound caustic soda. That process has since been replaced by more economical methods. However, sodium chloride is still widely used in the manufacture of other sodium compounds, especially sodium carbonate and sodium sulfate, in addition to sodium hydroxide. All four of these compounds, in turn, are used as raw materials in the manufacture of countless numbers of other products used in the production of paper pulp, synthetic fibers, textiles, dyes, processed foods, leather, water softeners, rubber, oil, metals, detergents, and glass and ceramics.

By far the largest use of potassium compounds is in the production of fertilizers. Smaller amounts are also used in specialized types of detergents, matches, explosives, photography, and glassware.

Lithium metal is used to make alloys with lead, magnesium, aluminum, and other metals. These alloys are strong and tough and find use in the manufacture of ball bearings, airplane parts, and armor plate. The most commonly used lithium compound is lithium stearate, a substance that changes oils into lubricating greases. Lithium carbonate (Li_2CO_3) is used in the manufacture of aluminum and in the production of special kinds of glass.

In 1949, researchers discovered that some lithium compounds are effective in treating manic-depressive disorders. They help control the wild swings of mood that are characteristic of this condition. A new and promising application for lithium is in the production of lithium-sulfur and lithium–iron sulfide batteries. These batteries may become efficient, nonpolluting substitutes for conventional lead storage batteries.

One of the better known applications of cesium is in an "atomic clock" that is used as the standard measurement of time throughout the world. Cesium hydroxide (CsOH) has been used as the electrolyte in an experimental fuel cell. Few uses have been found for rubidium metal or its compounds. One such compound, rubidium chloride (RbCl) has, however, been used medically as an antidepressant.

4

The Halogens

The elements that make up column 17 (VIIB) in the periodic table are known as the *halogen* family. The term *halogen* comes from two Greek words that mean "to form sea salt." The name was invented in 1811 by the German chemist J. S. C. Schweigger because chlorine, the first halogen discovered, was the first element found to combine directly with a metal to form a salt.

The halogens consist of a diverse group of elements. The first two, fluorine and chlorine, are highly reactive, poisonous gases. The third, bromine, is a deep red liquid, only one of two liquid elements. The fourth, iodine, is a gray, metallic-looking solid that, when heated, sublimes to form a beautiful violet vapor. The fifth, astatine, has no stable isotopes. It was first prepared synthetically in 1940 by D. R. Coreson, K. R. Mac Kenzie, and E. Segré. Since then, very small amounts have been detected in the earth's crust. But chemists believe that, overall, there is no more than about 45 milligrams on the planet, making astatine the rarest of all naturally occurring elements.

DISCOVERY OF THE HALOGENS

The first halogen to be isolated and studied was chlorine. In 1774, the Swedish chemist Carl Scheele added *spiritus salis* (hydrochloric acid [HCl]) to the mineral pyrolusite (manganese dioxide [MnO_2]) and obtained a pale green gas with a disagreeable, suffocating odor. He studied the properties of the gas and found that it bleached green leaves and flowers and reacted readily with metals. He had discovered chlorine, but did not realize that the gas—which he called *dephlogisticated marine acid*—was an element.

For nearly 40 years, chemists thought that Scheele's dephlogisticated marine acid was a compound. Then, in 1810, Sir Humphry Davy showed that the gas could not be reduced to anything simpler and named the new element *chlorine* (from the Greek *chloros*, for "pale green").

Very soon after Davy announced his discovery of chlorine, the second halogen was found. In 1811, the French chemist Bernard Courtois treated seaweed with concentrated sulfuric acid (H_2SO_4). In the reaction, he obtained a beautiful violet vapor that condensed to form a metallic-looking solid. When he could not decompose the solid, he decided that it must be an element. In 1813, the French chemist Gay-Lussac suggested the name *iodine* (from the Greek *iodes*, for "violet") for the element.

Credit for the discovery of bromine can be divided between two men, Carl Löwig and Antoine-Jerome Balard. Löwig first prepared the deep red liquid element in 1825 while a student at the University of Heidelberg. Before he could conduct studies of the substance, however, discovery of the new element was announced by Balard. Since Balard provided a complete description of the preparation and properties of bromine, he is usually acknowledged as the element's discoverer. The element's name (from the Greek *bromos*, for "stench") reflects one of its most obvious physical properties.

Compounds of fluorine were well known and widely used as far back as the seventeenth century. One *chemical compound*, fluorspar (calcium fluoride [CaF_2]), attracted attention because of its ability to emit light when heated. Another compound, hydrofluoric acid (HF), was widely used because of its ability to etch glass.

Another property of hydrofluoric acid is responsible for the tragic early history of fluorine. The gas is very poisonous and an extreme irritant to the skin and respiratory system. A number of scientists who worked with hydrofluoric acid, including Davy, Gay-Lussac, and Thenard, suffered serious injuries caused by working with the compound. Other researchers died as a result of their contact with the compound.

Little wonder, then, that fluorine itself was not isolated until relatively late. In 1886, the French chemist Henri Moissan obtained fluorine gas by *electrolysis* of a mixture of potassium hydrogen fluoride (KHF_2) and hydrofluoric acid. The name *fluorine* (from the Latin *fluere*, for "to flow") was proposed by A. M. Ampere in 1827. It reflects the early use of fluorspar as a flux.

OCCURRENCE OF THE HALOGENS

The halogens are all too active to occur free in nature. But some of their compounds are among the most common and most widely used by humans. Rock salt (sodium chloride [NaCl]), for example, is mentioned in some of the earliest written records. Its role in the human diet was recognized early and its value was acknowledged in its use as a form of money in some early cultures.

One compound of bromine is especially famous in history. The dye known as *Tyrian purple* is mentioned in the Bible and was well known to the Greeks and Romans. It is obtained from the tiny snail *Murex brandaris*. Since nearly 1,000 snails are required to extract a single gram of the compound, the dye was available only to royalty who could afford such an expense. In 1909, H. Friedlander showed that Tyrian purple was a compound of bromine.

Fluorspar was used as a flux as early as 1520 by the alchemist Georgius Agricola. Agricola explained that fluorspar was needed in the smelting of metals because "[it] caused the material in the fire to be much more fluid."

Fluorine is the most abundant of the halogens in the earth's crust. It is the thirteenth most common element, occurring to the extent of 544 ppm. Its most common mineral, fluorite (calcium fluoride [CaF_2]), is also the material from which the element is obtained commercially.

Chlorine and bromine rank twentieth and forty-sixth, respectively, in abundance in the earth's crust. The concentrations of the two elements are estimated to be 126 ppm for chlorine and 2.5 ppm for bromine. Both occur primarily as compounds of sodium and potassium (NaCl, KCl, NaBr, KBr) in the oceans and in salt beds formed by the evaporation of sea water.

Iodine is even less abundant (0.46 ppm) than its lighter halogen cousins, ranking sixtieth among the elements in the earth's crust. In the past, seaweed and nitrates from Chile were the main sources of iodine. Today, brine wells in the United States and Japan have become the primary sources of the element.

USES OF THE HALOGENS

The vast majority of fluorine produced today is used in the nuclear industry. The production of nuclear weapons and nuclear reactors requires that natural uranium be "enriched." That term means that the fraction of the uranium-235 isotope in a sample must be increased at least three or four times. In all commercial methods of enrichment currently used, the uranium is first converted to gaseous uranium hexafluoride, UF_6. The production of this compound accounts for more than 70 percent of all fluorine produced in the world.

The next most important use of fluorine is in the production of sulfur hexafluoride, SF_6. Because this gas is colorless, odorless, tasteless, stable, nontoxic, nonflammable, and unreactive, it is widely used as an insulator in high-voltage generators and other electrical equipment.

Chlorine has, for a number of years, ranked among the top ten chemicals produced in the world. It is the raw material used in the production of a host of other chemicals. The largest volume is used in the production of organic compounds used in medicines, dyes, synthetic fibers, pesticides, and other synthetic products. For example, the reaction of chlorine with ethylene results in the formation of vinyl chloride, the compound used in the manufacture of polyvinyl chloride (PVC), a widely used polymer.

About 10 percent of all chlorine produced is used to make inorganic chlorides, such as hydrochloric acid (HCl), aluminum chloride ($AlCl_3$), tin(IV) chloride ($SnCl_4$), arsenic(IV) chloride ($AsCl_4$), antimony(III) chloride ($SbCl_3$), titanium chloride ($TiCl_3$), zinc chloride ($ZnCl_2$), and mercury(I) chloride (Hg_2Cl_2). Finally, roughly one-fourth of all chlorine is used as a bleach or disinfectant, as in swimming pools and water purification and sewage treatment plants.

For many years, the major use of bromine was in "leaded" gasoline. A compound of bromine, ethylene dibromide, reacts with waste products formed during the combustion of leaded gasoline. Environmental concerns about lead have resulted, however, in a dramatic reduction in the production of leaded gasoline and, hence, in the demand for ethylene dibromide.

This decrease has been balanced to some extent by an increase in demand for other bromine compounds. Most prominent among these are pesticides. Methyl bromide, for example, is one of the most effective nematocides (worm-killers) known. Other compounds of bromine are in demand for the destruction of fungi, weeds, and other insect pests. The third most common application of bromine compounds is as flame retardants for clothing, carpets, and plastics.

Relatively small amounts of iodine are used in certain industrial processes (such as the manufacture of synthetic rubber), in dietary supplements for humans and other animals ("iodized" salt, for example), in dyes and pigments, in photographic film, and in drugs and medicines (tincture of iodine, as an example).

Portrait of French chemist Antoine Laurent Lavoisier (1743–1794). Lavoisier was one of the first to recognize the importance of accurate measurement in the analysis of chemical reactions. By careful weighing he showed that air is taken in by substances during combustion and, more generally, that any mass gained by one reactant is balanced by a loss elsewhere. This became known as the law of conservation of mass. He was the first to realize the nature of the combustion-supporting gas discovered by the English scientist Joseph Priestley and named it oxygen. In 1787 Lavoisier published a book that revolutionized chemical nomenclature by assigning every substance a name based on the elements of which it is composed.

Periodic Table

IA	IIA	IIIA	IVA	VA	VIA	VIIA		VI...
1 **H** 1.00794 Hydrogen								
3 **Li** 6.941 Lithium	**4** **Be** 9.01218 Beryllium							
11 **Na** 22.98977 Sodium	**12** **Mg** 24.305 Magnesium							

		3	4	5	6	7	8	9
19 **K** 39.0983 Potassium	**20** **Ca** 40.078 Calcium	**21** **Sc** 44.95591 Scandium	**22** **Ti** 47.88 Titanium	**23** **V** 50.9415 Vanadium	**24** **Cr** 51.9961 Chromium	**25** **Mn** 54.93805 Manganese	**26** **Fe** 55.847 Iron	**27** **Co** 58.933. Cobalt
37 **Rb** 85.4678 Rubidium	**38** **Sr** 87.62 Strontium	**39** **Y** 88.9059 Yttrium	**40** **Zr** 91.224 Zirconium	**41** **Nb** 92.9064 Niobium	**42** **Mo** 95.94 Molybdenum	**43** **Tc** (98) Technetium	**44** **Ru** 101.07 Ruthenium	**45** **Rh** 102.905 Rhodium
55 **Cs** 132.9054 Cesium	**56** **Ba** 137.327 Barium	**57** **La*** 138.9055 Lanthanum	**72** **Hf** 178.49 Hafnium	**73** **Ta** 180.9479 Tantalum	**74** **W** 183.85 Tungsten	**75** **Re** 186.207 Rhenium	**76** **Os** 190.2 Osmium	**77** **Ir** 192.22 Iridium
87 **Fr** (223) Francium	**88** **Ra** 226.025 Radium	**89** **Ac**** (227) Actinium	**104** **Unq** (261)† (Unnilquadium)	**105** **Unp** (262)† (Unnilpentium)	**106** **Unh** (263)† (Unnilhexium)	**107** **Uns** (262)† (Unnilseptium)	**108** **Uno** (265)† (Unniloctium)	**109** **Une** (266)† (Unnilnoniu...

*Lanthanide Series

58 **Ce** 140.115 Cerium	**59** **Pr** 140.9077 Praseodymium	**60** **Nd** 144.24 Neodymium	**61** **Pm** (145) Promethium	**62** **Sm** 150.36 Samarium

**Actinide Series

90 **Th** 232.0381 Thorium	**91** **Pa** 231.0359 Protactinium	**92** **U** 238.029 Uranium	**93** **Np** 237.048 Neptunium	**94** **Pu** (244) Plutonium

of the Elements

	IB	IIB	IIIB	IVB	VB	VIB	VIIB	NOBLE GASES

| | | | 13 | 14 | 15 | 16 | 17 | 18 |

| | | | | | | | | **2** **He** 4.00260 Helium | ⋆2 |

| | | | **13** | **14** | **15** | **16** | **17** | 2 8 |

| | | | **5** **B** 10.811 Boron | **6** **C** 12.011 Carbon | **7** **N** 14.0067 Nitrogen | **8** **O** 15.994 Oxygen | **9** **F** 18.998403 Fluorine | **10** **Ne** 20.1797 Neon |

| | | | **13** **Al** 26.98154 Aluminum | **14** **Si** 28.0855 Silicon | **15** **P** 30.973762 Phosphorous | **16** **S** 32.066 Sulfur | **17** **Cl** 35.4527 Chlorine | **18** **Ar** 39.948 Argon |

| 10 | 11 | 12 | | | | | | |

| **28** **Ni** 58.693 Nickel | **29** **Cu** 63.546 copper | **30** **Zn** 65.39 Zinc | **31** **Ga** 69.723 Gallium | **32** **Ge** 72.61 Germanium | **33** **As** 72.9216 Arsenic | **34** **Se** 78.96 Selenium | **35** **Br** 79.904 Bromine | **36** **Kr** 83.80 Krypton |

| **46** **Pd** 106.42 Palladium | **47** **Ag** 107.8682 Silver | **48** **Cd** 112.411 Cadmium | **49** **In** 114.82 Indium | **50** **Sn** 118.71 Tin | **51** **Sb** 121.757 Antimony | **52** **Te** 127.60 Tellurium | **53** **I** 126.9045 Iodine | **54** **Xe** 131.29 Xenon |

| **78** **Pt** 195.08 Platinum | **79** **Au** 196.9665 Gold | **80** **Hg** 200.59 Mercury | **81** **Ti** 204.383 Thallium | **82** **Pb** 207.2 Lead | **83** **Bi** 208.9804 Bismuth | **84** **Po** (209) Polonium | **85** **At** (210) Astatine | **86** **Rn** (222) Radon |

⋆ ⋆ Figures at extreme right indicate numbers of electrons in completed shell. (Figures in parentheses indicate numbers in incompleted shells.)

† The norms of elements 104–109 are recommended by IUPAC as systematic alternatives to those suggested by the purported discoverers.

This is a simplified form of the Sargent-Welch Periodic Chart. Catalog Number S-18805-50
Note: Atomic weight values given in parentheses indicate mass number of longest-lived (radioactive) isotopes.

| **63** **Eu** 151.965 Europium | **64** **Gd** 157.25 Gadolinium | **65** **Tb** 158.9253 Terbium | **66** **Dy** 162.50 Dysprosium | **67** **Ho** 164.9303 Holmium | **68** **Er** 167.26 Erbium | **69** **Tm** 168.9342 Thulium | **70** **Yb** 173.04 Ytterbiium | **71** **Lu** 174.967 Lutetium |

| **95** **Am** (243) Americium | **96** **Cm** (247) Berkelium | **97** **Bk** (247) Berkelium | **98** **Cf** (251) Californium | **99** **Es** (252) Einsteinium | **100** **Fm** (257) Fermium | **101** **Md** (258) Mendelevium | **102** **No** (259) Nobelium | **103** **Lr** (260) Lawrencium |

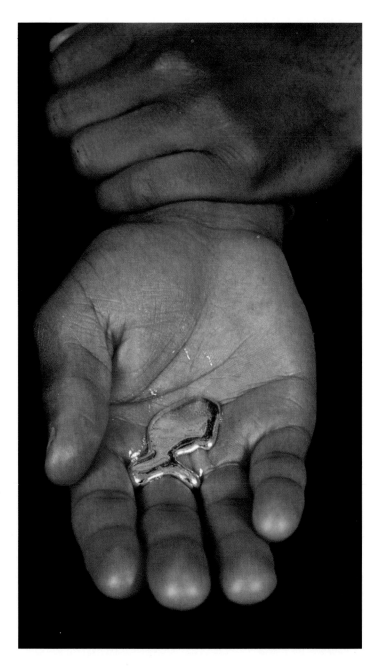

You would have trouble distinguishing a piece of gallium metal from silver, aluminum, and many other metals if they were all sitting next to each other on a shelf. But since it melts at 29.7°C (86°F), it becomes liquid in a person's hand, something no other solid metal will do.

Bromine is one of only two elements that is liquid at room temperature. It evaporates readily to form the beautiful reddish orange vapor shown here.

The element sulfur often exists underground in the form of this brilliant yellow solid known as rhombic sulfur.

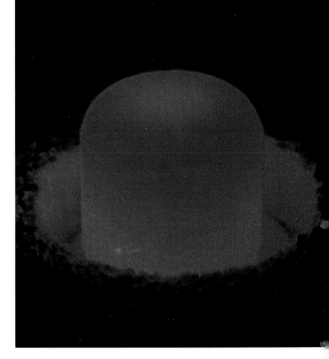

An element that does not occur naturally on the Earth, plutonium has taken its own picture here by means of the radiation it emits constantly.

As a solid, iodine is easily mistaken for a metal because of its bright, shiny luster. But when warmed, it sublimes and changes into the beautiful violet vapor shown in this photograph.

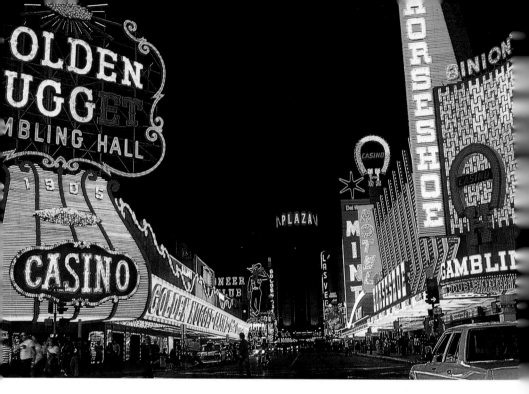

The brilliant colors that light up the skyline of Las Vegas are produced when electricity is passed through a gaseous element, such as neon, or the vapor of an element, such as mercury or sodium. "Neon" lights may actually contain any one inert gas or some combination of them.

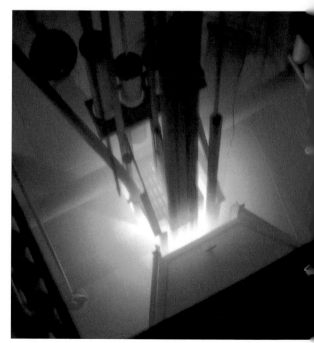

The cool blue glow in this photograph is produced by gamma rays given off by uranium, plutonium, or some other radioactive element used as a fuel in this nuclear reactor. The glow, called Cherenkov radiation, is produced when gamma rays from the radioactive element pass through water at a speed greater than the speed of light.

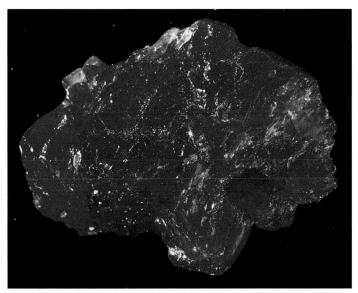

Above: *In its pure state, corundum is clear and colorless. When small amounts of the element chromium are incorporated into a corundum crystal, however, it then takes on the spectacular beauty of this ruby.*

Below: *One of the oldest and most widely used of all alloys is brass. The exact combination of copper and zinc—with perhaps small amounts of other metals—used in these tubas contributes to the distinctive musical tone they produce.*

Sulfur undergoes a series of interesting changes as it is heated. First, as its temperature increases, it changes from a yellow solid to an orange, and then a deep red, highly viscous liquid.

Below:
As heating continues, the tar-like liquid becomes more viscous. When poured into water, the sulfur turns back into a solid, this time a brown amorphous material that, after sitting for a few hours, reverts to its yellow solid state.

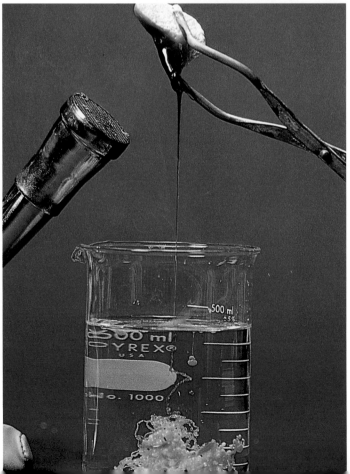

Sodium is a very active metal that reacts vigorously with water. The heat produced by this reaction is sufficient to metal sodium, which then forms a spherical body like the one shown here. The heat may also be sufficient to ignite hydrogen produced during the reaction. The pink color of the water in this photograph is caused by the presence of an indicator, a compound that detects the sodium hydroxide also formed in the reaction.

Copper is not a particularly reactive element. But concentrated nitric acid is strong enough to attack the metal, producing blue copper sulfate and clouds of noxious, brown nitrogen dioxide gas.

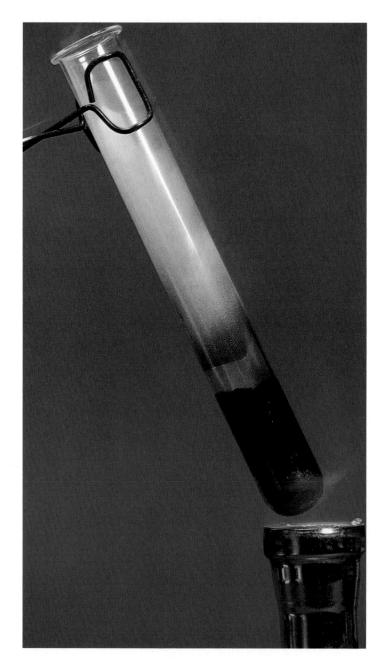

Under the proper conditions, most metals will react with most nonmetals. In this case, the heating of iron with sulfur results in the formation of iron (II) sulfide, also known as ferrous sulfide, a grayish compound. The color you see in the test tube is excess sulfur being evaporated and burned off as sulfur dioxide.

 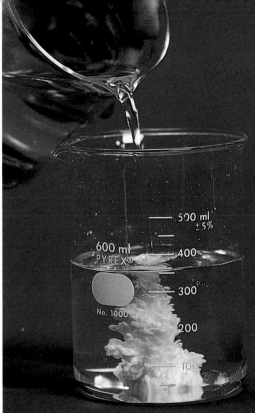

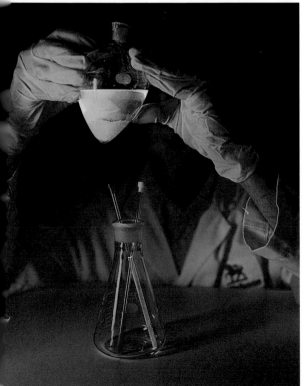

Above left:
The solutions in the two beakers shown here—potassium iodide in the upper beaker and lead nitrate in the lower beaker—are both colorless . . .

Right:
. . . but the reaction of these two compounds produces a new substance, lead iodide, that is yellow.

Fluorescent chemicals, like the one being used by this chemist, are more than just interesting curiosities. Because they continue to glow in the dark after being exposed to light, they can be used to "track" an element in chemical research.

The riot of colors in Yellowstone National Park's Morning Glory
hot springs pool results from the accumulation of various elements
in the water and rocks surrounding the pool. Iron, manganese,
chromium, and other metals, for example, provide tints of red,
orange, yellow, and green in rocks and minerals that would
otherwise be dull brown, gray, or black.

Spectacular new architectural forms, like the "harp" design of Tampa Bay's Sunshine Skyway Bridge, are made possible by tough, strong, long-lasting alloys that contain titanium, vanadium, molybdenum, chromium, and many other metals little known to most of us.

Below:
The chalk (calcium carbonate) that makes up the White Cliffs of Dover is all that remains of the shells of countless numbers of marine microorganisms that died and sank to the bottom of ancient seas.

Glassmaking is one of the oldest chemical arts known to humans. The presence of trace elements—probably cobalt, iron, and manganese in this photograph—has been responsible for the variety of colors that craftspersons have been able to achieve in their work.

5

Hydrogen and the Noble Gases

HYDROGEN

In many ways, hydrogen is a very special element. This special character is sometimes indicated by the way it is placed in the periodic table, with its own box, slightly displaced from the alkali metals and the rest of the chemical elements. That is, while similar to the alkalis in some ways, it is also unique among the elements in many other ways.

Hydrogen atoms are the simplest of all atoms. Each consists of a single proton and a single electron. One of the most famous theories of chemical history was that of William Prout (1758–1850). Prout suggested that hydrogen was the building block of which all other elements are formed. Prout's hypothesis was eventually rejected, but it contained a kernel of truth. Scientists believe that the formation of all elements in the universe does begin by the combination (fusion) of hydrogen atoms at the center of stars. Also, every element can be identified by the number of protons (hydrogen nuclei) its atoms contain.

In addition to the most common form of hydrogen atom, consisting of one proton and one electron, two other *isotopes* of hydrogen exist. The atoms of *deuterium* contain one proton, one electron, and one neutron, while those of *tritium* contain one proton, one electron, and two neutrons. To distinguish the most common form of hydrogen from its heavier isotopes, it is sometimes called *protium*.

Discovery of Hydrogen

Hydrogen was prepared and studied long before it was recognized as an element. In 1671, for example, Robert Boyle added dilute sulfuric acid to iron and obtained "copious and stinking fumes" (hydrogen) that burned "with a blueish and somewhat greenish flame." Similar experiments were conducted with similar results by a number of chemists over the next century.

Finally, in the 1760s, the English chemist Henry Cavendish carried out a series of experiments on hydrogen and provided a complete description of the gas's properties. He had some incorrect ideas as to where the element comes from and what it really is. Making use of an old, but still popular theory, Cavendish referred to the gas as *dephlogisticated air*. In spite of these misunderstandings, Cavendish is generally given credit for having discovered the element. Its modern name was given it by Lavoisier in 1783 because of its role in the formation of water (*hydro-* = "water" and *-gen* = "formation of").

The heavier isotopes of hydrogen were not discovered until the twentieth century. In 1932, Harold Urey, at Columbia University, allowed 4 liters of liquid hydrogen to evaporate until only a few milliliters remained. In examining this residue spectroscopically, Urey found two faint lines that indicated the presence of "heavy hydrogen," or deuterium.

The third isotope, tritium, was first prepared synthetically in 1934 by M. L. E. Oliphant, P. Harteck, and E. Rutherford. Five years later, tritium was found to be a *radioactive isotope*, and 15 years later, it was first detected in the earth's *atmosphere*.

Occurrence of Hydrogen

Hydrogen is the most abundant and versatile element in the universe. Of every 1,000 atoms in the universe, 886 are hydrogen. It is less common on earth, but still makes up one of every six or seven atoms on the planet. Hydrogen is, of course, the most abundant atom by far in the earth's *hydrosphere* (oceans, lakes, rivers, and other bodies of water). On the basis of weight, it is the ninth most abundant of the elements, occurring to the extent of about 0.9 percent.

Protium is by far the most common isotope of hydrogen (99.9844 percent); the concentration of deuterium amounts to only 0.0156 percent. The natural concentration of tritium in the atmosphere is estimated to be no more than 10^{-6} percent.

Hydrogen forms compounds with more different elements than does any other element. It undergoes *chemical reactions* with nonmetals and metalloids to form hundreds of different acids, including hydrochloric acid (HCl), sulfuric acid (H_2SO_4), nitric acid (HNO_3), phosphoric acid (H_3PO_4), and hydrocyanic acid (HCN). It also reacts with metals to form two-element compounds known as hydrides. Hydrogen also occurs in all bases, such as sodium hydroxide (caustic soda [NaOH]), potassium hydroxide (KOH), calcium hydroxide (slaked lime [$Ca(OH)_2$]), and magnesium hydroxide ($Mg(OH)_2$). Hydrogen is also a component of almost every organic compound.

Uses of Hydrogen

One of hydrogen's most characteristic properties is that it burns with a pale blue, very hot flame. This property has made it useful in specialized torches such as the oxyhydrogen torch that can produce flames with temperatures of about 2,300° C. Many chemists, hoping to make greater commercial use of this property, talk about a "hydrogen economy" in which hydrogen replaces coal, oil, and natural gas as the most important fuel for human society. One of the great advantages of a hydrogen economy is that the combustion of hydrogen creates as its final product only water, a harmless substance that poses no threat to the environment. At the present time, the technology for making and using hydrogen as a commercial fuel is too expensive to allow the development of a hydrogen economy.

The largest single use of hydrogen today is in the production of ammonia, a compound that generally ranks about second among all industrial chemicals produced in the United States. Large amounts of hydrogen are also used in the catalytic hydrogenation process that converts liquid oils into solid fats. The element is also a raw material in the production of metal hydrides and organic compounds. Smaller quantities of hydrogen are used in rocket fuels and in bubble chambers used as detectors in particle accelerators.

THE NOBLE GASES

When Mendeleev developed his first periodic table in 1869, there was no column 18 (VIII), and for good reason: None of the elements that make up that family had yet been discovered. Ironically, the first member of that family, helium, had actually been discovered in that same year (1869), but its existence was not confirmed for another three decades.

As the members of this family were gradually discovered between 1894 and 1898, an interesting property was observed for them all: They appeared to be chemically inert. Their inability to form compounds with other elements prompted chemists to call the members of this group the inert, (or noble) gases. The term *noble* suggests that the elements are too "proud" to become involved with other chemical elements.

By the 1960s, it became obvious that the noble gases were not totally inert. Compounds of at least one of them (xenon) had been prepared, and there was reason to believe that others could also be made to react. Thus, the family is no longer referred to as the inert gases.

Discovery of the Noble Gases

The first noble gas to be observed was discovered not on earth, but in the sun. In 1868, the French astronomer Pierre Jules César Janssen noticed a previously unidentified line in the solar spectrum during a total eclipse of the sun. The English astronomer Sir Norman Lockyer suggested that the line might belong to a new element, which he named *helium* (from the Greek *helios*, for "sun").

Over the next quarter century, scientists agreed that the new element might occur in the sun, but that it probably did not exist on the earth. In 1881, however, the Italian chemist L. Palmieri observed the same spectral line in a substance taken from Mount Vesuvius. Even then, it was not until 1895 that Sir William Ramsay was able to produce and identify helium from the mineral cleveite and confirm that the element did exist on the earth.

Ramsay had also been responsible for the discovery of the first noble gas found on earth, argon, in 1894. More than a century earlier, Cavendish had commented on the fact that, after removing both oxygen and nitrogen from air, a small fraction of unidentified gas remained. His determination that this unidentified gas had a volume of "$1/120$ part of the whole" was remarkably accurate even if he was unable to determine what the gas was. He did suggest that it might be a new element.

Scientists ignored or forgot Cavendish's discovery until nearly the end of the nineteenth century. Then, the English physicist Lord Rayleigh made a discovery similar to that of Cavendish. He found that nitrogen gas prepared by three different methods had slightly different densities. The resolution to this problem was provided by Ramsay, who showed that some samples of Rayleigh's "nitrogen" actually contained a new element, while others did not. The new element was soon named *argon* (from the Greek *argos*, for "inactive").

The discoveries of helium and argon made clear the need for a new column in the periodic table. They also indicated that additional elements must exist to fill the gaps in the new column. In rapid succession, three more noble gases were discovered by the fractional distillation of liquid air: *krypton*, on May 30, 1898; *neon* in June of the same year; and *xenon* on July 12, 1898. Two years later, the final member of the family, *radon*, was discovered as a product of radioactive decay by the German chemist Friedrich Ernest Dorn.

Occurrence of the Noble Gases

Helium is the second most abundant element in the universe, accounting for 113 of every 1,000 atoms. It is much less abundant on earth, where it occurs to the extent of 5.24 ppm in air and about 10^{-3} ppm in the earth's crust. In contrast, argon is relatively abundant in the atmosphere, with a concentration of 93.40 ppm, the third most common gas. Neon is the next most abundant noble gas (18.18 ppm), followed by krypton (1.14 ppm), xenon (0.087 ppm), and radon (variable small amounts).

No naturally occurring compound of a noble gas has ever been observed. The belief that no such compound *can* exist was disproved only in 1962 when the British chemist Neil Bartlett produced the mixed salt xenon hexafluoroplatinate, $XePtF_6$. Within a few months, two more compounds, xenon difluoride (XeF_2) and xenon tetrafluoride (XeF_4), had also been announced. Over the following 30 years, a number of other compounds of xenon and krypton were made. No stable compounds of helium, neon, or argon, however, have yet been announced.

Uses of the Noble Gases

Most applications of the noble gases depend on their non-reactivity. For example, important historical documents are sometimes stored in enclosed cases in an atmosphere of argon to protect them from decay (oxidation). Also, helium is used in dirigibles (to a much more limited extent than previously) because it is nonflammable. Argon is also used to fill incandescent lamp bulbs because it will not react with—and hence, damage—the bulb filament when it is heated.

The first five noble gases are also used in "neon" and fluorescent lamps. The color produced by such lamps depends on the gas or combination of gases in the lamp (in "neon" lamps) or on the coating used in the lamp (in fluorescent lamps). The noble gases are also used in low-temperature research, as coolants in some types of nuclear reactors, and in deep-sea diving systems.

6 Some Common Metals

Most people have a reasonably accurate understanding of the term *metal*. That understanding is probably not so different from the technical definition. A metal is any substance that has a lustrous surface, is malleable (can be hammered into thin sheets) and ductile (can be drawn into thin wires), and conducts heat and electricity. Metals also have some common chemical properties. For example, they tend to react with nonmetals to form salts and they tend to react with water to form bases.

In spite of these common characteristics, individual metals have some interesting distinctive properties. Mercury, for example, is the only liquid metal. Iron, cobalt, and nickel are the only strongly magnetic metals. Cesium is the softest of all metals with a melting point lower than body temperature. Radium, polonium, thorium, uranium, and some other metals are radioactive. That is, these metals give off radiation spontaneously and change into a new element.

It should be obvious that this book can provide no more than a general overview of the 80-odd metals in the periodic table. The emphasis in this chapter, therefore, will be on important generalizations and specific information of special interest. Two special groups of metals—the lanthanides and actinides—are the subject of Chapter 7.

DISCOVERY OF THE METALS

Some of the best-known metals—gold, silver, copper, iron, tin, lead, and mercury—were well known to ancient cultures. The first six are all mentioned in the Old Testament. The discovery of methods for making bronze (an alloy of copper and tin) in about 3500 B.C. was so important that it gave its name to a whole era of human history, the Bronze Age. The widespread use of iron implements some 2,500 years later resulted similarly in the rise of a period known as the Iron Age.

Evidence for the existence of gold, silver, and copper for use as coins, in jewelry, and as decorations goes back to at least 5000 B.C. The coffin of Tutankhamun (died about 1350 B.C.), for example, is decorated with more than 100 kg of gold. Lead was used in some cultures for coins and by the Romans for water pipes, cooking utensils, and writing tablets. The first two uses were unfortunate since they undoubtedly contributed to widespread lead poisoning among the Romans.

Mercury was undoubtedly as intriguing an element to the ancients as it is to today's beginning chemistry student. Early alchemists often attributed special powers to the element that, as the great alchemist Paracelsus wrote, "is a fluid, but does not moisten, and runs about, though it has no feet." Some natural philosophers even claimed that mercury was one of the few truly basic elements.

Probably the first metal discovered since ancient times is zinc. The thirteenth century Indian manuscript *Rasarnava* describes a method for making zinc from calamine. The method apparently passed to China, where zinc was described in a 1637 book entitled *Tieng kong kai ou*. By that time, the metal was commonly used for coins by the Ming emperors.

During the next 150 years, an additional dozen metals were discovered: cobalt in 1737, platinum in 1748, nickel in

1751, manganese and barium in 1774, molybdenum in 1778, tungsten in 1781, uranium and zirconium in 1789, strontium in 1790, titanium in 1791, and chromium in 1797. The nineteenth century saw a flood of discoveries, as most of the remaining 60-odd metals were added to the list of new elements.

In some cases, two or more elements were found in association with each other and/or at nearly the same time. Platinum was mentioned by an Italian visitor to Central America as early as 1557; however, the metal was not recognized as an element until 1748. When techniques for working with platinum ores were refined at the beginning of the nineteenth century, however, four more metals were quickly identified in those ores. The English chemist William Hyde Wollaston discovered palladium and rhodium in platinum ores in 1803–4, and his contemporary, Smithson Tenant, discovered osmium and iridium over the same two-year period.

The chemical similarity of two or more metals has sometimes meant that they are difficult to separate from each other and, hence, difficult to recognize as two distinct elements. For example, the English chemist Charles Hatchett discovered the metal niobium in 1801. (In an interesting dispute, the element was first named *columbium*, a name that is still used by many scientists in the United States for the element.) A year later, the Swedish chemist Anders Ekeberg announced the discovery of a second element, very similar to niobium and found in conjunction with it, an element he called tantalum.

In 1809, however, the eminent and widely respected Wollaston announced that his research showed that niobium and tantalum were actually identical and that Ekeberg's discovery was invalid. Chemists accepted this view for nearly four decades until the German chemist Heinrich Rose showed that Wollaston was wrong, Ekeberg was right, and niobium and tantalum really are distinct elements. The complexity and confusion that can arise as the result of similar properties is nowhere as obvious as in the case of the rare earth elements, which are described in Chapter 7.

Finally, a handful of metals were prepared synthetically before they were ever observed in the earth. Technetium and promethium are two examples. Moseley's discovery of atomic numbers in 1913 made it possible to predict with near certainty the number of elements still to be discovered. By the mid-1930s, two obvious gaps remained in the periodic table, elements number 43 and number 61. All efforts to locate these elements in nature failed, however. Chemists began, instead, to investigate methods for producing these elements artificially.

The first success was achieved in 1936, when E. Segré and C. Perrier at the University of Palermo discovered a new element—number 43—in the products of a reaction carried out originally at the University of California's cyclotron. The discoverers gave the name *technetium* (from the Greek *technetos*, for "artificial") to the element.

A decade later, the last missing element was produced. While examining the products of a *nuclear fission* reaction, J. A. Marinsky, L. D. Glendenin, and C. D. Coryell, at the Oak Ridge National Laboratories, found evidence for element 61. They named the element *promethium* after the mythological Greek god Prometheus, who stole fire from heaven for human use. The techniques used by the Palermo and Oak Ridge teams were soon extended to the search for elements heavier than the heaviest natural element, uranium. The results of that search are described in Chapter 7.

OCCURRENCE OF THE METALS

The most abundant metal in the earth's crust is aluminum, ranking number 3 overall behind oxygen and silicon. Its estimated concentration is 83,000 ppm. Following in order after aluminum are iron (number 4: 62,000 ppm), calcium (number 5: 46,600 ppm), magnesium (number 6: 27,640 ppm); sodium (number 7: 22,700 ppm), potassium (number 8: 18,400), titanium (number 9: 6,320 ppm), and manganese (number 12: 1,060 ppm). The abundance of other metals ranges from about 380 to 390 ppm (barium and strontium) to a low of less than 0.01 ppm. The least common metals are estimated to be osmium (0.005 ppm), gold (0.004 ppm), iridium and tellurium (0.001 ppm), rhenium (0.0007 ppm), and ruthenium and rhodium (0.0001 ppm).

Because they tend not to react with other elements, some metals occur most commonly or always in their native state. These include gold, silver, platinum, ruthenium, osmium, rhodium, iridium, and palladium. During the great gold rush of the 1840s in California, miners often picked up nuggets of pure gold worth thousands of dollars lying on the bare ground. Platinum was first seen by European colonists when they found nuggets of the pure metal that had been washed down from mountains by rivers and streams.

Most metals occur combined with other elements in simpler or more complex compounds. For example, some of the metals that occur as the oxide are iron (hematite [Fe_2O_3] and magnetite [Fe_3O_4]), titanium (rutile [TiO_2]), zirconium (baddeleyite [ZrO_2]), and manganese (pyrolusite [MnO_2] and hausmannite [Mn_3O_4]). A few that occur combined with sulfur are iron (pyrites [FeS_2]), zinc (sphalerite [ZnS]), mercury (cinnabar [HgS]), copper (chalcocite [Cu_2S]), and cobalt (linnaeite [Co_3S_4]).

Examples of metals that occur in more complex compounds include aluminum (kaolinite [$Al_2(OH)_4Si_2O_5$]), magnesium (dolomite [$MgCa(CO_3)_2$] and talc [$Mg_3Si_4O_{10}(OH)_2$]), nickel (garnierite [$(Ni,Mg)_6Si_4O_{10}(OH)_8$]), and tungsten (powellite [$Ca(Mo,W)O_4$]).

USES OF THE METALS

The metallic elements have thousands of applications in industry and everyday life. One way to classify those

45

applications is according to the form in which the metal occurs: in its native (uncombined) state, as an alloy, or as a compound with other elements.

Uses of the Pure Metals

Some metals have special properties that make them useful in their native state. One of the most familiar examples may be the use of mercury in clinical thermometers. As the only liquid metal, mercury has properties of expansion and contraction that can be used as a simple and accurate indication of temperature change. Chrome plating is another common example of the use of a metal's special properties. Chromium is much more resistant to oxidation than is iron. Covering iron with a thin layer of chromium not only protects the iron but adds an attractive, shiny finish to the metal.

Tungsten metal is strong and has a very high melting point (more than 5,000° C), so it makes an ideal material to use as the filament in an incandescent light bulb. The color, luster, stability, and rarity of gold, silver, and platinum have led to their use in coins and jewelry throughout human history. The ability of copper to conduct electricity with very little resistance accounts for the fact that the major use of this metal is in wires and electrical equipment.

Pure metals have also found extensive use as catalysts in the chemical industry. A *catalyst* is a material that speeds up or slows down a chemical reaction without undergoing any change itself. Most car owners are aware of the fact that their automobile's exhaust system contains a catalytic converter, a device that removes undesirable gases from the car's exhaust. That catalytic converter is likely to contain metallic platinum.

Platinum and other platinumlike metals are also used in other industrial processes, such as the production of nitric acid, the refining and reforming of petroleum, the conversion of oils to fats, and other specialized chemical reactions. A combination of platinum and rhenium is now used in the manufacture of gasoline that is low in lead, a process that accounts for nearly 100 percent of all the rhenium produced in the United States.

Uses of Metallic Alloys

An *alloy* is a mixture of two or more elements with properties that make it useful in industry, in research, or for other purposes. Hundreds of different alloys with an enormous variety of properties and applications are known. The peculiar property of some alloys is illustrated by an alloy of indium and gallium that is liquid at room temperature. In contrast, alloys of tantalum tend to be very strong, with very high melting points, making them useful as pen points and in specialized chemical instruments.

Steel is perhaps the most familiar of all alloys. Steel is produced by alloying iron with metals such as chromium (to form hard, stainless steel), molybdenum (stainless steel used in high-speed tools), manganese (present in all kinds of steel), vanadium (wear-resistant steel that retains its strength at high temperatures), niobium (stainless steel that remains strong at high temperatures), and nickel (very strong steel used for armor plating).

The challenge for a chemical researcher is to find out exactly which metals to combine and how much of each to use to obtain an alloy with the exact properties desired. For example, M. G. Corson discovered in 1926 that the addition of beryllium to copper increases its strength by about 600 percent without affecting its electrical properties. Chemists have also developed alloys of magnesium, aluminum, zinc, and manganese that weigh much less than do steel alloys of the same strength, but that can be worked more easily. These alloys are in demand, therefore, for aircraft bodies, luggage, optical equipment, and similar applications.

Less familiar metals also form some interesting and useful alloys. For example, yttrium is a primary component of Misch metal, a pyrophoric substance. A pyrophoric substance is one that makes a spark when it is scratched.

Because of this property, Misch metal is used in cigarette lighter flints. Indium metal, combined with bismuth, cadmium, lead, and tin, forms a low-melting-point alloy that can be used in automatic fire extinguishers, heat regulators, and other safety devices. Niobium and zirconium can be alloyed to make wires used in superconducting magnets.

One of the most famous of all alloys is alnico, which gets its name from the three metals that make it up, *al*uminum, *ni*ckel, and *co*balt. Alnico is used in the manufacture of electromagnets that are twenty-five times more powerful than conventional steel magnets. Alloys of the platinum metals (platinum, palladium, rhodium, iridium, osmium, and ruthenium) are very hard and very resistant to other chemicals. That property makes them desirable for use in chemical and electrical instruments and in jewelry.

Two applications of alloys that have become increasingly important in recent years involve the nuclear industry and medical technology. A number of alloys are now used in nuclear power plants because they tend to speed up or slow down nuclear reactions. For example, alloys of cadmium and hafnium are used in control rods because they absorb neutrons efficiently, thereby slowing down the fission process. These alloys are also very strong and resistant to corrosion. Alloys of zirconium, in contrast, are used in metal coating for reactor rods because they have a very low tendency to absorb neutrons. The contrasting properties of hafnium and zirconium present an interesting problem for scientists since the two elements are so chemically similar that they are difficult to separate from each other. But, because they have opposite functions in a nuclear power plant, total separation of the two is vitally important.

For many years, special steel alloys were used in the construction of artificial knees and hips, as pins and rods to hold bones together, and for replacement of other body parts. Scientists eventually discovered, however, that other alloys may be even better for these purposes. Today, medical prostheses are often made of tantalum alloys because they are chemically inert, do not react with body fluids or tissues, and are at least as strong as steel.

Uses of Metallic Compounds

The number of metallic compounds with important commercial uses runs into the hundreds. Some of the most familiar are those used in construction. Steel is, of course, one of the most important modern building materials. But naturally occurring compounds of calcium and magnesium were used for thousands of years before steel was invented. Limestone and marble, both forms of calcium carbonate ($CaCO_3$), were used for construction at least as far back as the ancient Egyptians and Babylonians. Gypsum, alabaster, and plaster of Paris—all forms of calcium sulfate ($CaSO_4$)—are other building materials used by both ancient and modern cultures.

In 1824, an English bricklayer, Joseph Aspdin, invented an artificial building material called *Portland cement*. Portland cement is made by heating limestone, sand, and clay together. The product is a very strong, rocklike material that is not affected by water. U.S. production of Portland cement now exceeds 75 million tons per year.

Another category of complex metallic compounds known for centuries is the *ceramics*. The term *ceramic* refers to a material fashioned out of clay or some other natural earth at room temperature that is then hardened permanently by heating. Bricks, bowls, dishes, cups, and other household items are frequently made of ceramics.

The development of new types of ceramics is one of the most exciting fields of research today. Scientists are discovering ways to alter the raw materials and methods of production to make ceramics with a whole host of unusual and useful properties. Among the new ceramic products that have been developed or are under study are magnetic ceramics, ceramics strong enough to be used in jet rocket nozzles, ceramic knives and scissors, fuel cells and automobile engines made of ceramics, and glasslike ceramics that can be used as cookware. Probably the single most important application of these new-age ceramics is in the electronics industry, where they are used to insulate and support integrated circuits.

Another use of metallic compounds that goes far back in human history is as dyes and pigments. Many compounds have colors that can be used to tint glass, ceramics, enamels, and even bricks. Beads, pottery, and glass dyed with blue compounds of cobalt have been found among Egyptian and Persian artifacts that date to 2000 B.C. and beyond. Cinnabar, the red ore of mercury, was also used by ancient artisans to color materials. "Ruby gold," so called because its red color was similar to that of the gemstone ruby, was used by alchemists of the Middle Ages.

The colored compounds of tin, chromium, manganese, cobalt, copper, nickel, iron, and other metals are also widely used as pigments in modern society. For many years, compounds of lead were in high demand because of their vivid colors: red (lead tetroxide [Pb_3O_4]), yellow (lead monoxide [PbO] and lead chromate [$PbCrO_4$]), orange (lead molybdate [$PbMoO_4$]), white (white lead [2 $PbCO_3 \cdot Pb(OH)_2$]), and black (lead sulfide [PbS]). These compounds have fallen into disuse for most applications, however, because of their serious toxicity. For many purposes, lead pigments have been replaced by compounds of other metals. For example, the most important single use of titanium dioxide (TiO_2) today is in the manufacture of white paint.

A number of metallic compounds are used for specialized pigments. For example, tin compounds are used in the manufacture of ceramics to add colors such as pink (a mixture of SnO_2 and Cr_2O_3), yellow (SnO_2 and V_2O_5), and blue-gray (SnO_2 and Sb_2O_5). Phosphorescent paints, containing pigments that glow in the dark, are made from zinc sulfide (ZnS), which produces a yellow, orange, or green glow; or copper(II) sulfide (CuS) or strontium sulfide (SrS), which produce a bluish glow. Colored compounds of chromium

(Cr_2O_3), titanium (Ti_2O_3 and TiO_2), and cadmium (CdS) are added to some types of paints to make them heat-resistant. Manganese dioxide (MnO_2) is used in the brick-making industry to produce tints that range from gray to brown to red.

Metallic compounds occur in living systems in very low concentrations. For example, the human body contains no more than 5 mg of cobalt. Yet these metallic compounds play crucial roles in the maintenance of health in the human body. Cobalt, for example, apparently occurs in only one form in living organisms, as part of a compound called *cobalamin*, or *vitamin B₁₂*. This vitamin is necessary to prevent the condition known as *pernicious anemia*. Humans take in sufficient quantities of vitamin B_{12} in a normal diet. When absorption does not occur normally, or under other circumstances, a person may have to take vitamin B_{12} supplements.

Other metals that occur in living systems include magnesium (necessary for nerve impulses, muscle contraction, and carbohydrate metabolism), calcium (for formation of teeth and bones and for blood clotting), iron (for transport of oxygen), copper (for maintenance of healthy blood cells and carbohydrate metabolism), and zinc (for protein metabolism and transport of carbon dioxide). Magnesium is also crucial in the plant world as a component of chlorophylls, compounds that initiate the process of photosynthesis.

On the other hand, a number of metals are toxic to living organisms. Chromium, mercury, lead, beryllium, cadmium, and nickel are among these. Mercury(II) chloride ($HgCl_2$), for example, has long been used as a poison known as *corrosive sublimate*. The use of mercury compounds in the manufacture of felt hats was responsible for a medical condition known as "hatter's shakes," and for the expression "mad as a hatter." Both conditions are caused by the mercury-induced degeneration of the nervous system. In 1952, the accidental ingestion of food contaminated with methyl mercury (CH_3Hg) resulted in the death of fifty-two people in Minamata, Japan.

51

New uses for metallic compounds are constantly being discovered. Since the discovery of radioactive isotopes, for example, medical researchers have been finding more and more uses for radioactive metals. One of the most commonly used isotopes is technetium-99m. This isotope can be produced quickly and easily in the very location where it is to be used from a "molybdenum cow." The "cow" produces technetium-99m continuously for radioactive tracer diagnosis procedures.

The discovery of semiconductors and their applications in solid state electronics has also opened a whole new field for metallic compound research. Chemists have learned that certain compounds of aluminum, gallium, germanium, and indium have properties that make them useful in special kinds of transistors. Indium phosphide (InP), for example, is now being used in transistors that must operate at high temperatures, while indium arsenide (InAs) and indium antimonide (InSb) are used in low-temperature transistors. The compound gallium arsenide has the ability to convert electricity directly into light. It is used, therefore, in the production of light-emitting diodes (LEDs) that make up the "read-out" on watches and clocks, computers, and other electronic devices.

The invention of synthetic inorganic fibers illustrates yet another line of research. These materials, made of aluminum oxide (Al_2O_3) and zirconium oxide (ZnO_2), can be drawn into very long fibers with very uniform thickness, high tensile strength, and a soft, silky feel. Researchers predict that they will find applications in yarns, cloth, blankets, rugs, rope, fiber mattes, and many types of paper- and cardboardlike materials.

7 The Lanthanides and Actinides

Two groups of metals of special interest are the lanthanides and actinides. They consist of the fourteen elements each that occur in the middle of rows 6 and 7 of the periodic table (which are usually printed separately at the bottom of the table). Each group is named after the element that precedes it in the periodic table, lanthanum or actinium.

Both groups are also known by other designations. The lanthanides were long known as the rare earth elements. The older name is somewhat misleading since the elements in this group are not particularly rare. They are, however, very similar to each other chemically and, therefore, very difficult to separate from each other.

The actinides include the three heaviest naturally occurring elements, thorium, protactinium, and uranium, and eleven synthetically produced elements. Because of their position in the periodic table, these eleven elements are often called the transuranium elements.

DISCOVERY OF THE LANTHANIDES

Anyone who enjoys a good mystery story will be fascinated by the early history of the rare earth elements. That history began in 1787 when a Swedish military officer, Carl Axel Arrhenius, found an unusual black rock in a quarry near the town of Ytterby, Sweden. In 1794, the Finnish scientist,

John Gadolin, investigated the black mineral found by Arrhenius and found that it contained about 38 percent of a new oxide. Later investigators assigned the names *gadolinite* to the black mineral, in honor of Gadolin, and *yttria* to the new oxide in it, after the name of the town where it was found.

A second new mineral had been discovered in Sweden in 1751, this one near the town of Bastnäs. No one paid much attention to this "heavy stone of Bastnäs" until 1803, however. Then, the German chemist Martin Klaproth and the Swedish chemists Jöns Jacob Berzelius and Wilhelm Hisinger independently discovered the presence of another new oxide in the mineral. The name *cerite* was given to the mineral and *ceria* to the new oxide in it. For a time, scientists thought that the end result of this story was that two new elements—yttrium and cerium—had been discovered.

In fact, the story had not ended, but was just beginning. Over the next century, dozens of chemists analyzed the two new "elements" and found that each was a complex material containing seven (in the case of ceria) and nine (in the case of yttria) new elements. Three of these sixteen new elements—yttrium, lanthanum, and scandium—are not themselves rare earth elements although they are chemically related to the family.

Rather than retell the complex and confusing story of these discoveries, we offer the chart on pages 56 and 57, which shows the sequence and dates of discoveries, the names of the discoverers, and the origins of the elements' names. The only lanthanide missing from this chart is promethium, discovered in 1945 among the products of a nuclear fission reaction.

OCCURRENCE OF THE LANTHANIDES

Contrary to their common name, the lanthanides are not especially rare. Cerium and neodymium rank numbers 26 and 27, respectively, in abundance in the earth's crust, ahead of better known metals such as lead (number 36), tungsten (number 55), and mercury (number 64). The least common lanthanide, promethium, is found only in trace amounts and only in ores of uranium.

More than 100 minerals are known to contain the lanthanides, but only two have very much commercial importance, monazite and bastnaesite. Cerium, praseodymium, and neodymium (along with the closely related, but non-lanthanide lanthanum) make up the largest fraction of lanthanides in these two ores.

USES OF THE LANTHANIDES

For many years, the problem of separating the lanthanides from each other limited their commercial use. The one commercially important product was a naturally occurring mixture of lanthanide oxides, Misch metal, that requires relatively little processing. The pyrophoric properties of Misch metal were described on page 53. Misch metal has also been used in the production of steel alloys, where it improves the workability and strength of the steel.

In recent years, chemists have found a number of new uses for the lanthanide metals. A number of their compounds are used, for example, as phosphors in color television sets. When struck by an electron beam, these phosphors glow with characteristic colors: green for salts of terbium and red for salts of europium, yttrium, and erbium. Neodymium oxide (Nd_2O_3) is used in color television tubes to improve contrast and brightness.

An alloy of samarium and cobalt ($SmCo_5$) has been used to make the most powerful electromagnets yet produced. Dysprosium and europium are sometimes used in control rods in nuclear reactors because of the elements' strong tendency to absorb neutrons. Another unusual use for europium salts is in the manufacture of postage stamps, a technique that makes possible electronic scanning of the stamps.

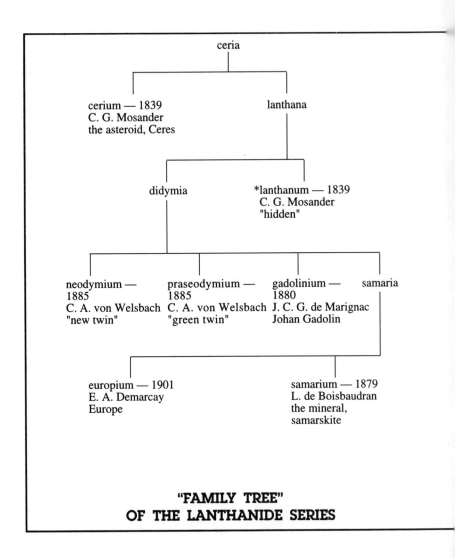

ceria

cerium — 1839
C. G. Mosander
the asteroid, Ceres

lanthana

didymia

*lanthanum — 1839
C. G. Mosander
"hidden"

neodymium —
1885
C. A. von Welsbach
"new twin"

praseodymium —
1885
C. A. von Welsbach
"green twin"

gadolinium —
1880
J. C. G. de Marignac
Johan Gadolin

samaria

europium — 1901
E. A. Demarcay
Europe

samarium — 1879
L. de Boisbaudran
the mineral,
samarskite

"FAMILY TREE"
OF THE LANTHANIDE SERIES

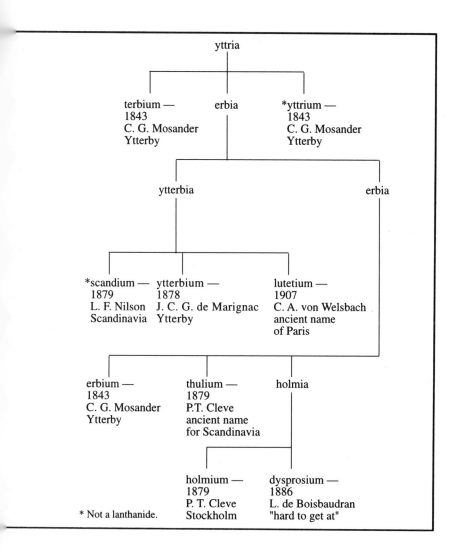

yttria

terbium —
1843
C. G. Mosander
Ytterby

erbia

*yttrium —
1843
C. G. Mosander
Ytterby

ytterbia

erbia

*scandium —
1879
L. F. Nilson
Scandinavia

ytterbium —
1878
J. C. G. de Marignac
Ytterby

lutetium —
1907
C. A. von Welsbach
ancient name
of Paris

erbium —
1843
C. G. Mosander
Ytterby

thulium —
1879
P.T. Cleve
ancient name
for Scandinavia

holmia

* Not a lanthanide.

holmium —
1879
P. T. Cleve
Stockholm

dysprosium —
1886
L. de Boisbaudran
"hard to get at"

In the form of its oxide, cerium is used to coat the inner walls of self-cleaning ovens and is used to polish glass. Even the rarest lanthanide, promethium, has found a few limited applications. It has been used on watch dials, in highly specialized paints, and in auxiliary power units on space vehicles.

DISCOVERY OF THE ACTINIDES

Of the fourteen actinide metals, one—uranium—stands out in importance. Indeed, because of its role in nuclear weapons and nuclear reactors, it can be said to have changed the face of human civilization over the past 50 years. The metal was first discovered by Martin Klaproth in 1789, although some of its compounds had been used as far back as at least 79 A.D. Klaproth named the element after the recently discovered planet Uranus.

For a century after Klaproth's discovery, uranium was of relatively little interest to chemists, and they found few uses for it or its compounds. Then, in 1896, the French physicist Henri Becquerel discovered the property of uranium—radioactivity—that was to make its place in history.

Thorium was discovered by Berzelius in 1829. He named the element after the Scandinavian god Thor. As with uranium, the metal's radioactivity was not discovered until much later (1898). Protactinium, the third of the naturally occurring actinides, was not discovered until 1913 when Kasimir Fajans and O. H. Göhring identified the element among the decay products of uranium-238. Fajans and Göhring's original name for the element, *brevium*, was intended to illustrate its short *half-life.* The name was later changed, however, first to *protoactinium*, and then to *protactinium*, or "parent of actinium."

The remaining eleven elements in the actinide family were all produced originally by artificial means. The general technique is to bombard uranium or one of the heavier elements with neutrons, *alpha particles*, or other particles in a particle accelerator or nuclear reactor. If the target nucleus captures one or more of these particles, it is converted to a new nucleus of another, heavier element.

The preparation of the first transuranium element, neptunium, is an example. When a uranium-238 nucleus is bombarded with neutrons, it captures a neutron and changes into a slightly heavier nucleus, uranium-239. The new nucleus is unstable and decays by emitting a beta particle. The *beta particle* is produced within the uranium nucleus when a neutron changes into a proton and an electron (the beta particle). The presence of a new proton converts the uranium nucleus into a new nucleus with an atomic number one greater than that of uranium, 93. The new element thus formed was named *neptunium* by its discoverers, Edwin McMillan and Philip Abelson, in 1940 since the planet Neptune is next to Uranus in the solar system, and the new element is next to uranium in the periodic table.

Similar techniques, using heavier and heavier "bullets," have been used by chemists to produce all of the actinide metals. The new elements have been named after the place where they were first produced (americium, berkelium, and californium), after famous scientists (curium, einsteinium, fermium, mendelevium, nobelium, and lawrencium), and, in the case of plutonium, after the last of the planets.

OCCURRENCE OF THE ACTINIDES

Thorium (8.1 ppm) and uranium (2.3 ppm) are, respectively, the thirty-ninth and forty-seventh most abundant elements in the earth's crust. Protactinium is so rare as to be unmeasurable for all practical purposes. Although prepared originally by synthetic means, minute amounts of neptunium and plutonium are produced by natural neutron bombardment of uranium minerals in the earth's crust. The only source of the other transuranium elements is reactions that occur in particle accelerators and nuclear reactors.

The primary source of thorium is the mineral monazite, which may contain up to 20 percent of thorium oxide (ThO_2). Pitchblende and carnolite are the two most common uranium-bearing ores, although neither contains more than about 0.1 percent of the metal itself.

USES OF THE ACTINIDES

Compounds of uranium once found use as toners in photography, as mordants in the dyeing of silk and wool, in color glazes for pottery and dishes, and in the leather industry. It is used almost exclusively today, however, in the production of nuclear weapons and in nuclear reactors for peacetime uses.

The most common application of thorium today is in the manufacture of Welsbach mantles used in portable gas lanterns. When heated with a gas flame, a Welsbach mantle emits a brilliant white light. Thorium oxide is also used in the manufacture of high-quality glass and as a catalyst in various industrial processes. Given the greater abundance of thorium than uranium, some scientists anticipate that techniques may some day be developed to allow the metal to be used in place of uranium in nuclear reactors.

Of the transuranium elements, only plutonium has found extensive commercial use. The isotope plutonium-239 is produced in large quantities in conventional uranium reactors and can, itself, be used as a fuel in other types of reactors. Except for neptunium, no other transuranium element exists in large enough quantity to have other than modest commercial use. Our knowledge of the chemical and physical properties of the last four actinides comes from the analysis of no more than a handful of atoms and, in the case of lawrencium, of only a single atom.

A few exceptions to the preceding statement involve americium, which is used as an ionization source in smoke detectors; curium, which has been used in small, compact power sources for space vehicles; and californium, which has been used in the treatment of cancer and in the determination of water- and oil-bearing layers in petroleum exploration.

8 The Nonmetals

The nonmetals constitute a much smaller group of elements than the metals, no more than about fifteen elements in all. Two of the families already discussed, the halogens and noble gases, make up two-thirds of the nonmetals. The remaining nonmetals include some of the most interesting and commercially important of the elements, however. These are carbon, nitrogen, oxygen, phosphorus, and sulfur.

DISCOVERY OF THE NONMETALS

Two of the nonmetals—carbon and sulfur—were well known to the ancients. References to coal, asphalt, bitumen, petroleum, and natural gas—all forms of carbon—have been found from biblical times. For example, a Greek historian of the fourth century B.C. tells of a natural gas well in Turkey that provided a perpetual flame for religious ceremonies. Many reports also tell about the practice of mixing lampblack, a form of carbon, with olive oil and balsam gum to make a primitive form of ink. Diamonds, another form of carbon, are described in the Bible and in some ancient Hindu manuscripts.

Sulfur is also mentioned in many early manuscripts, often as brimstone. The term *brimstone* was sometimes used to describe sulfur itself, but more often to describe any flammable substance. Numerous passages in the Bible mention "fire and brimstone" as a means for bringing destruction upon evil people and cities. Some early philosophers thought that sulfur and mercury, or at least the qualities that they represented, were the two basic elements of nature. By Roman times, writers were consistently talking about the mining of sulfur and its use in matches, lamp wicks, explosives, bleaches, and medicines.

Compounds of phosphorus had been familiar to early philosophers primarily because of their fascinating tendency to glow in the dark (phosphorescence). The element itself was not isolated, however, until the 1660s. Then, the German alchemist and physician Hennig Brand allowed a large sample of human urine to putrify for many days before distilling the product. He was surprised and delighted to find in the distillate a small amount of waxy white material that glowed in the dark: pure phosphorus.

The discovery of nitrogen in 1772 is usually credited to Daniel Rutherford, a Scottish botanist, chemist, and physician. While studying for his doctor of medicine degree under Joseph Black, Rutherford was assigned the task of studying the gas that remains after carbon-containing substances burn in air. Rutherford's thesis described methods by which this gas (nitrogen) could be prepared and summarized many of its properties. Some controversy surrounds the crediting of Rutherford's discovery, however. Scheele, Cavendish, and Priestley all isolated nitrogen at about the same time as did Rutherford. Furthermore, Rutherford did not claim that the gas he studied was an element, but thought that it was ordinary air saturated with *phlogiston*. Indeed, the elemental nature of nitrogen was not completely accepted until the midnineteenth century. The element's name was suggested by Jean-Antoine-Claude Chaptal in 1790. The name comes from two Greek words that refer to nitrogen compounds (*nitron*) and "origin" (*gen*).

The history of oxygen's discovery goes back at least 1,200 years. The earliest reference may be one in an eighth-century Chinese book that relates the yin to one part of air (oxygen) and the yang to the other part (nitrogen). In Western Europe, the first person to realize that air consists of two distinct parts was Leonardo da Vinci in the fifteenth century. Recognition of oxygen as a distinct elementary gas was made simultaneously in the early 1770s by Joseph Priestley in England and Carl Scheele in Sweden. The true nature of oxygen as an element was not fully appreciated, however, until Lavoisier studied the gas in 1775. Out of Lavoisier's studies came the modern theory of combustion as being a chemical reaction in which some material combines with oxygen. In enunciating this theory, Lavoisier sounded the death knell for the phlogiston theory of combustion.

OCCURRENCE OF THE NONMETALS

Oxygen is the most abundant element on earth, making up 46 percent of the earth's crust by weight, 23 percent of the atmosphere, and 86 percent of the hydrosphere. The oxygen-rich atmosphere that makes life on earth possible is a relatively new phenomenon in earth history. The planet's earliest atmosphere probably consisted primarily of methane, hydrogen, carbon monoxide, and other "reducing" gases. Only after green plants appeared about 2.5 billion years ago, did oxygen begin to appear in the atmosphere, and it probably did not reach its present concentration until about 580 million years ago. Oxygen is also abundant in crustal rocks in the form of oxides, carbonates, silicates, and phosphates.

Nitrogen is by far the most common gas in the atmosphere, about four times as abundant as oxygen. It occurs much less commonly in the earth's crust, however, and is essentially absent from the hydrosphere. Its abundance in crustal rocks is estimated to be about 19 ppm, making it the thirty-third most abundant element in the *lithosphere*. The two most important nitrogen-containing minerals are saltpeter (potassium nitrate [KNO_3]) and Chilean saltpeter (sodium nitrate [$NaNO_3$]).

The second most abundant nonmetal is phosphorus.

With an estimated concentration of 1,120 ppm, it ranks eleventh in abundance in the earth's crust, followed by sulfur (340 ppm, sixth) and carbon (180 ppm, seventeenth). Almost all of the minerals of phosphorus are phosphates, including a large number that make up the *apatite* minerals. The apatites include calcium, phosphate, and one or more halogens. Phosphorus also occurs in low concentrations in living organisms, where it carries out a number of important functions.

Sulfur sometimes occurs in the elemental form and can be mined directly, like coal. The appearance of brilliantly yellow sulfur caps on top of salt domes is truly a spectacular sight. Sulfur also occurs widely as metallic sulfides. Some familiar examples include galena (lead sulfide [PbS]), pyrites (iron sulfide [FeS_2]), sphalerite (zinc sulfide [ZnS]), cinnabar (mercury(II) sulfide [HgS]), chalcopyrite (a mixed sulfide of iron and copper [$CuFeS_2$]), chalcocite (copper(I) sulfide [Cu_2S]), and greenockite (cadmium sulfide [CdS]).

Carbon occurs both as a *native* element (graphite and diamond, for example) and in combined form (carbon dioxide, metallic carbonates, and organic compounds). The relatively low concentration of carbon in crustal rocks gives no indication of its enormous importance on the planet. While carbon dioxide makes up only a minor part of the atmosphere (about 330 ppm), for example, the compound makes possible the survival of all green plants and, hence, of all animal life on earth. In addition, the number of *organic* (by definition, carbon-containing; versus *inorganic*) *compounds* runs into the millions, accounting for about 90 percent of all compounds known to science.

All of the nonmetals, except nitrogen, exist in two or more forms known as *allotropes*. One of the best examples of allotropism is found in carbon, which may occur as a soft black crystalline material, graphite; a hard crystal, diamond; or a black solid or powder without crystalline structure (charcoal and carbon black, respectively).

The allotropes of oxygen include the familiar dioxygen

(O_2) as well as ozone (O_3) and atomic oxygen (O). A thin layer of ozone in the earth's upper atmosphere captures incoming ultraviolet radiation, protecting animals on earth from its harmful effects. There is now some concern about possible damage to this layer caused by human activities, with the resultant threat that it may pose for life on earth.

Phosphorus exists in at least five crystalline and several *amorphous* (noncrystalline) allotropic forms. The most common of these is the waxy white solid discovered by Brand. Other well-known allotropes exist as purple or black crystalline forms or as red or black amorphous forms.

Sulfur exists in more allotropic forms than any other element. This property results from the ability of sulfur atoms to combine with each other in long chains or in rings. The allotropes are represented by symbols that indicate the number of sulfur atoms in the chain or ring. For example, the most common allotrope is the yellow crystalline material produced commercially as flowers of sulfur, milk of sulfur, or sulfur roll, S_8. Other allotropes range in color from pale yellow (S_{12} and S_{20}) to red (S_3 and S_6) to bluish purple (S_2).

USES OF THE NONMETALS

The vast majority of sulfur produced is converted into sulfur dioxide (SO_2), which, in turn, is used to make either sulfuric acid (H_2SO_4) or sulfurous acid (H_2SO_3). Sulfuric acid consistently ranks as the most widely produced industrial chemical in the world, its total volume often exceeding that of the next two chemicals combined. The acid's importance results from its use as a raw material in the manufacture of other chemicals, such as fertilizers (about half of all sulfur use), synthetic detergents, gasolines, synthetic plastics, dyes, medicines, pesticides, paints and enamels, synthetic fibers, tires, photographic film, explosives, and storage batteries.

The production of paper pulp from sulfurous acid accounts for about 3 percent of all sulfur produced. A small amount of elemental sulfur is used in the production of insecticides and medicines and in rubber vulcanization, and some sulfur dioxide is used as a refrigerant and bleach.

The primary applications of elemental nitrogen depend upon its relatively low tendency to react with other substances. For example, it is used as an inert gaseous "blanket" in the iron and steel industry, where exposure to oxygen can cause fires and explosions. The petrochemical and electronics industries employ nitrogen gas for similar purposes.

Compounds of nitrogen have a large variety of commercial and industrial uses. In fact, four such compounds— ammonia (NH_3), nitric acid (HNO_3), ammonium nitrate (NH_4NO_3), and urea (($NH_2)_2CO$)—are normally among the fifteen chemicals produced in largest volume in the United States. By far their most important application (more than 80 percent of all nitrogen produced) is in the manufacture of fertilizers. Explosives and synthetic fibers are two other important products of nitrogen compounds. A number of other nitrogen compounds produced in smaller volume have some minor, but interesting uses. Magnesium and sodium nitrates ($Mg(NO_3)_2$ and $NaNO_3$), for example, are used in the manufacture of long-lasting flares and photoflash devices.

Elemental phosphorus has relatively few practical uses. One group of applications depends on the tendency of white phosphorus to catch fire easily and to burn with the release of large amounts of dense white smoke. Because of this property, white phosphorus is used in smoke bombs, tracer bullets, and incendiary shells.

At least 80 percent of all phosphorus produced each year is converted to phosphoric acid (H_3PO_4) and the remainder to other compounds of phosphorus. Phosphoric acid is by far the most important of all phosphorus compounds, usually ranking about ninth on the list of chemicals produced in the United States. About 95 percent of all phosphoric acid produced is used in the manufacture of fertilizer. The remaining 5 percent is used in the treatment of metals (about 20 percent) and in the production of other phosphorus compounds (about 80 percent). These "other" compounds of phosphorus have many practical applications, including the production of synthetic detergents, paint strippers, food additives, toothpastes, baking powder and baking soda, fireproofing agents, enamels, ceramics, and additives for stock feeds.

One of the most interesting uses of a phosphorus compound was discovered in 1916 by J. L. Kraft. Kraft found that the addition of a small amount of dibasic sodium phosphate (Na_2HPO_4) during the production of pasteurized cheese greatly improved the efficiency of that process. Kraft's discovery, in modified form, is still widely used in the commercial production of processed cheese. Another well-known compound of phosphorus is phosphorus sesquisulfide (P_4S_3), used in the manufacture of "strike anywhere" matches. The friction of this type of match sets off a chemical reaction between phosphorus sesquisulfide and a second compound, potassium chlorate ($KClO_3$), that results in a spark and flame.

The industrial demand for elemental oxygen has increased dramatically in the last 50 years, largely as a result of its use in the production of iron in blast furnaces and of steel in the Bessemer process. Over the last decade, these uses have placed oxygen in the top five among chemicals produced in largest volume in the United States. The gas is also used in the smelting of many metals, manufacture of glass, high-temperature welding and cutting, and the production of other chemicals. A relatively minor, but well-known use of oxygen is as an oxidant in rocket fuels, such as those used to propel the space shuttle. A very large number of oxygen compounds are known. Their uses have been mentioned in early chapters of this book.

A satisfactory review of the uses of carbon and its compounds would require a complete book at least the size of this one. Perhaps its best known allotrope, diamond, has long been in demand in the manufacture of jewelry. As the hardest known naturally occurring substance, however, diamond has also had a number of industrial uses, as in devices for the drilling, polishing, grinding, and cutting of other materials. Dies used in the manufacture of tungsten and other hard wires and parts for delicate instruments, for example, are often made of diamond.

So valuable and desirable has diamond been in human society that scientists have long tried to manufacture synthetic diamonds from other forms of carbon. Not until 1954, however, were those efforts successful. Then, Percy Bridgman found a method for subjecting graphite to temperatures of more than 2,000° C and pressures of more than 20,000 atmospheres. Under these conditions, Bridgman was able to produce a number of very tiny diamonds that had no value as jewelry, but could be put to use in industrial applications. Today, Bridgman's techniques have been improved to the point where one-carat diamonds can now be made synthetically.

Graphite, a less glamorous allotrope of carbon, is used in the manufacture of "lead" pencils, pigments, lubricants, electrodes for carbon-arc lamps and electrochemical cells, and moderators in nuclear reactors. A new process makes possible the growth of carbon "whiskers," long, thin threads of pure graphite. These whiskers can be interwoven with thread or embedded in plastics, metals, or other substances to produce strong, tough materials.

Yet a third allotrope, amorphous carbon, is used in deodorizing and decolorizing of materials; in inks, dyes, and pigments; in electrical equipment; and in some medicines. One form of amorphous carbon, carbon black, can be produced in the form of a very fine powder known as *activated carbon*. Because the particles of activated carbon are so small, the total surface area of even a small sample of the substance is enormous. This large surface area makes activated carbon useful as a material for adsorbing (adhering) other substances. About a third of all activated carbon produced is used to remove unwanted color during the manufacture of white sugar.

70

Carbon has one property that sets it off from all other elements. Its atoms have the ability to combine with themselves in an almost infinite variety of ways. They can form long chains that contain hundreds or thousands of atoms, sometimes with side branches and sometimes not. They can form "cyclic" molecules that contain one or more rings, or they can form structures that look like boxes, cages, chains, or other objects. The *chemical formulas* shown in Figure 2 illustrate some of these structures.

The apparently endless versatility of carbon accounts for the number of different compounds it forms. In fact, a whole field of chemistry—organic chemistry—is devoted solely to the study of carbon compounds. The number of compounds that contain carbon is probably about ten times that of all noncarbon compounds.

Most of the compounds that make up living organisms are organic compounds. These include sugars, starches, cellulose, fats, waxes, oils, hormones, enzymes, and nucleic acids. The last of these, the nucleic acids, are the chemicals that carry genetic information stored in cells. They tell cells what functions they are supposed to perform.

In the last half decade, scientists have learned how to change the genetic information stored in nucleic acids. This field of research is known as *genetic engineering* or *recombinant DNA research* (DNA is the acronym for deoxyribonucleic acid). The possible applications of genetic engineering are nearly limitless. Scientists have already learned, for example, how to make tobacco plants that have a natural resistance to certain pests, how to increase the amount of milk given by a cow, and how to cure certain inborn disorders of humans.

One of the most productive lines of chemical research is the production of synthetic organic compounds. Each year, chemists create hundreds or thousands of new organic compounds. The majority of these are invented without any practical application in mind. But many are soon put to use in some part of our daily lives.

71

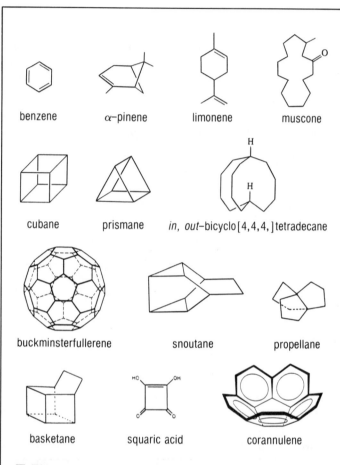

benzene   α–pinene   limonene   muscone

cubane   prismane   *in, out*–bicyclo[4,4,4]tetradecane

buckminsterfullerene   snoutane   propellane

basketane   squaric acid   corannulene

■ **Figure 2.** *Some organic molecules. These diagrams are simplified representations of complex chemical formulas. In each formula, a carbon atom is assumed to be present at the intersection of two or more lines, and a hydrogen atom is assumed to be attached to each carbon atom.*

One class of synthetic organic compounds with which everyone is familiar is the plastics. The first plastics were invented more than 100 years ago. Today, hundreds of different kinds of plastics—such as the polyethylenes, the polypropylenes, polystyrenes, poly(vinyl chlorides), methyl methacrylates, and polyesters—are known.

Any list of the way plastics are used would be incomplete, but would include packaging materials, sports equipment, squeeze bottles, insulation, car and boat bodies, synthetic rubber, fibers, paints, adhesives, contact lenses, gaskets, toys, carpeting, phonograph records, coolers, nonstick coatings, piping, coating for textiles, sealants, caulking, dyes, and glass substitutes.

One of the most interesting new forms of plastic is made from the compound known as polyacetylene. When a small amount of iodine is added to this plastic, it becomes electrically conductive. Chemists are intrigued by the applications that might be made from a plastic that conducts electricity. It is conceivable that your car's battery will someday be made out of such a material that could be produced in the form of thin sheets lining the interior of the car hood.

Another whole area of research in organic chemistry involves the development of better drugs and medicines. Chemists have learned how to "tailor-make" certain compounds that have very special biological properties. They can manufacture synthetic materials, for example, that mimic the effects of naturally occurring drugs but that do not have harmful side effects characteristic of the natural product.

Many synthetic organic compounds are a mixed blessing for society. Although they may have desirable commercial applications, they often, at the same time, pose health or environmental hazards. The insecticide known as dichlorodiphenyltrichloroethane (DDT) is an example. Invented in 1939 by the German chemist Paul Müller, DDT eventually proved to be one of the most effective insecticides ever discovered. It was eventually put to use in dozens of ways by farmers and public health workers between 1942 and the 1970s. Then, the adverse environmental effects of the chemical resulted in its ban in most countries of the world.

The DDT story illustrates at once two aspects of the successful search by chemists for new synthetic products. On the one hand, these products can bring about remarkable improvement in the health, safety, and general satisfaction of human society. On the other hand, they may also create unexpected and staggering environmental, social, political, ethical, and economic questions for the society.

9 The Metalloids

Many versions of the periodic table contain a diagonal line that runs down the right side of the table, separating the metals from the nonmetals. The elements on either side of the diagonal lines are called the *metalloids* or *semimetals*. Elements classified as metalloids are boron, silicon, germanium, arsenic, antimony, tellurium, polonium, and astatine. The metalloids are so named because they have the properties of both metals and nonmetals.

DISCOVERY OF THE METALLOIDS

Compounds of some metalloids were certainly known to ancient peoples. Arsenic compounds, for example, were sometimes used as dyes and pigments. Their most common use, however, was as poisons. Chinese farmers have used arsenic compounds for centuries to kill rats and insects that attack their crops and food stores. Most cultures have been aware of the poisonous quality of arsenic compounds. Greek and Roman records, for example, describe the high death rate among slaves who were forced to work in arsenic mines.

Compounds of antimony are described in biblical records. Writers tell of women who use "stibic stone," probably antimony(III) sulfide (Sb_2S_3), to paint their faces. Women in other cultures have apparently also used compounds of antimony as an eyeliner to make their eyes appear larger and more striking.

Ancient civilizations had apparently learned how to make glassware from quartz, sand, and other compounds of silicon at least as far back as 1250 B.C. In some passages of the Bible, writers equated the value of "fine crystal" with that of gold.

The first two metalloids to be recognized as elements were arsenic and antimony, discoveries that came as a result of research in *alchemy* in the Middle Ages. The great German scholar Albertus Magnus is sometimes given credit for having first isolated arsenic in the thirteenth century. But there is no conclusive evidence to support this claim, and most scholars were unclear about the elemental nature of arsenic until the studies of J. F. Henckel and Georg Brandt in the 1720s and 1730s.

Antimony was also recognized as an element by the alchemists, but it was often confused with one of its compounds. Its history is so confused that no one person can be given credit for its discovery although Jean-Baptiste Buquet is usually acknowledged as the person who suggested its modern name.

Although borax (sodium tetraborate [$Na_2B_4O_7$]) was known to the ancients and used by them in the making of glass, the element itself was not isolated until 1808. Then, L.-J. Gay-Lussac and L.-J. Thenard in France and Humphry Davy in England decomposed boric acid to obtain elemental boron. Neither research team was able to purify the element, however, and it was not until 1892 that Henri Moissan was able to produce boron that was more than 95 percent pure. The name boron was suggested by Davy to show its source (*bor*ic acid) and its similarity to carb*on*.

The first descriptions of tellurium occurred in the mid-eighteenth century. The Hungarian chemist Joseph Ramacsaházy wrote about a substance (tellurium) that appeared to be "unripe gold." That term refers to an alchemical theory that metals grow in the earth in much the same way that plants and animals do. The final stages of metal growth were thought to be silver, then gold. Ramacsaházy wrote that he wanted to find a method for "ripening" his discovery in order to obtain pure gold.

The true nature of the element was discovered by Baron Franz Joseph Müller von Reichenstein, who had, nonetheless, some trouble making up his mind on the matter. He first announced in 1782 that Ramacsaházy's "unripe gold" was bismuth sulfide (Bi_2S_3). Later, he changed his mind and decided that the substance was really a new element, which he named after the Latin word *tellus*, for "earth." It was not until 1796, however, that Klaproth was able to confirm that Baron von Reichenstein had really discovered the new element.

The true nature of silica (silicon dioxide [SiO_2]), found in sand, quartz, and other common minerals, eluded chemists for centuries. The major difficulty is that silicon bonds so tightly to oxygen that it is very difficult to decompose the compound they make up, silica. Finally, in 1824, Berzelius was able to isolate relatively pure silicon from potassium fluosilicate (K_2SiF_6). The element's name was suggested by Thomas Thomson to show its origin (*silica*) and its similarity to carb*on*.

The discovery of germanium by C. A. Winkler in 1886 has special significance in the history of chemistry. In 1871, Mendeleev had predicted the existence of an element needed to fill an empty space beneath silicon in his periodic table. Mendeleev predicted with amazing accuracy the properties to be expected of this *eka*silicon. Working with Mendeleev's predictions as a guide, Winkler discovered the missing element in a recently discovered ore of silver, sulfur, and mercury. Winkler suggested the name *germanium* for the new element in honor of his homeland, Germany.

The other two elements predicted by Mendeleev were also named for their discoverers' native lands, scandium (for Scandinavia, by Nilson) and gallium (for Gaul, Latin for France, by Boisbaudran). The remarkable match between the predicted and the observed properties of germanium is illustrated in the following table.

Property	Ekasilicon (Es)	Germanium (Ge)
Atomic weight	72	72.32
Atomic volume	13	13.22
Valence	4	4
Specific gravity	5.5	5.47
Specific heat	0.073	0.076
Specific gravity of the dioxide	4.7	4.703
Molecular volume of the dioxide	22	22.16
Boiling point of the tetrachloride	less than 100° C	86° C
Specific volume of the tetrachloride	1.9	1.887
Molecular volume of the tetrachloride	113	113.85

The two remaining metalloids, polonium and astatine, both occur only as radioactive isotopes. The former was discovered in 1898 by Marie Curie and named in honor of her homeland, Poland. Astatine was first prepared by D. R. Corson, K. R. MacKenzie, and E. Segré in 1940 and named after the Greek word for "unstable."

OCCURRENCE OF THE METALLOIDS

Silicon is the most abundant of the metalloids and the second most common element in the earth's crust (after oxygen). It makes up 27.2 percent of the earth's crust by weight. It is less common in the earth's core and mantle and much less common in the universe as a whole. The primary compounds of silicon are silicon dioxide (SiO_2) and a large variety of silicates, such as olivine, pyroxene, mica, feldspar, amphibole, and zeolite.

The other metalloids rank fairly low in abundance. Boron is next most common in the earth's crust (number 38: 9 ppm), followed by arsenic (number 51: 1.8 ppm), germanium (number 53: 1.5 ppm), antimony (number 62: 0.2 ppm), and tellurium (number 72: 0.001 ppm). The total amounts of polonium and astatine have been estimated at 2,500 metric tons and 44 milligrams, respectively.

Probably the most familiar boron-containing mineral is borax, or sodium tetraborate ($Na_2B_4O_7$). It and related minerals appear to form during the evaporation of hot springs. They tend to be found, therefore, in areas of volcanic activity. One such site, at Boron, California, covers an area of nearly 10 square kilometers to a depth of 25 to 50 meters.

Two of the most common ores of arsenic, orpiment and realgar, were known to the Greeks and Romans. Both are sulfides of arsenic (orpiment = arsenic trisulfide [As_2S_3]; realgar = arsenic disulfide [As_4S_4]) and, along with the oxide (arsenolite [As_2O_3]), are the main sources of arsenic today. The most important ore of antimony, stibnite (antimony trisulfide [Sb_2S_3]), was also known to the ancients and was used by them to color glass.

Germanium occurs primarily in the native state, mixed with ores of zinc. It is recovered and produced commercially during the roasting of those ores. Tellurium occurs in the elemental state, mixed with silver and gold, and in the combined state as tellurides and the oxide (tellurite [TeO_2]). Tellurium-containing minerals are so rare, however, that the element is obtained primarily as a by-product (along with silver and gold) in the refining of copper metal.

USES OF THE METALLOIDS

Boron is a versatile element, forming hundreds of compounds with novel and interesting structures. The vast majority of these compounds have no commercial application or are used only in chemical research. The family known as the borates are used in making special types of glasses, detergents, cosmetics, enamels, pesticides, and fertilizers. Another group of boron compounds, the borides, are known for being very hard, chemically inert, and good conductors of electricity. Some have melting points of more than 3,000° C. Some members of this group are boron carbide (B_4C), chromium boride (CrB_2), titanium boride (TiB_2), hafnium boride (HfB), zirconium boride (ZrB_2), and niobium boride (NbB).

Some applications of the borides include their use in turbine blades, rocket nozzles, and linings for combustion chambers and high-temperature furnaces. A technique has also been developed for making fibers out of boron carbide and then using those fibers in the manufacture of bulletproof clothing. Because of the element's ability to absorb neutrons very efficiently, another important application of the borides is in control rods in nuclear power plants.

Both arsenic and antimony have long been used in a variety of alloys. For example, Geoffrey the Elder, an early-eighteenth-century writer, described the use of antimony in making bells, tools, and type for printing presses. Even today, about half of all the antimony produced is used in making alloys. The most common of these alloys is one with lead used in storage batteries. The addition of antimony to lead improves its hardness and strength. Other alloys of antimony are used in the manufacture of bearings, ammunition, solder, and type metal. The last of these uses depends on a somewhat unusual property of antimony. As its liquid alloys are cooled, they tend to expand, rather than contract. Thus, when the liquid alloy is poured into a mold, it expands to fill every part of the mold, producing type that has clean, crisp edges.

Arsenic is also used in alloys, especially with lead and copper. The addition of arsenic to lead and copper shot, for example, improves their tendency to form perfectly spherical drops. Both arsenic and antimony are used in the production of compounds important in the electronic industry, including light-emitting diodes (LEDs) used in pocket calculators and wristwatch displays, specialized types of lasers, and infrared detecting devices.

Compounds of arsenic were once widely used as pesticides. However, concerns about their environmental effects have caused a cutback in their production for this purpose. Fair amounts are still used under controlled conditions, however, as pesticides, wood preservatives, and dips for cattle and sheep and in the tanning of leather. Antimony compounds can be found in paints and dyes, matches, ceramics, fireworks, percussion caps, and fireproofing materials. It is interesting to note that, while most compounds of antimony are toxic, one, tartar emetic (antimony potassium tartrate $[K(SbO)C_4H_4O_6]$), has long been used as a medicine.

Tracing the many uses of silicon and its compounds is a truly staggering task. Simply to mention the various naturally occurring forms of silicon compounds—sand, clay, quartz, diatomaceous earth, mica, talc, asbestos, and kaolin—suggests the enormous range of the element's uses. The simplest of these compounds, silica (silicon dioxide), is used in the manufacture of glass, ceramics, enamels, and abrasives. Increasing volumes are used as a food additive to prevent the caking of powdered materials in preprocessed foods. Quartz, one form of silica, is most widely used in the manufacture of a variety of electromechanical devices.

Over the past century, chemists have invented a number of synthetic compounds of silicon with special properties that make them commercially valuable. One such compound is silicon carbide (SiC), also known as *carborundum*. Carborundum is one of the hardest materials known to science and finds applications, therefore, in devices for cutting, polishing, and smoothing materials. For many industrial purposes, it is cheaper and equally efficient to use carborundum in place of diamonds for these purposes. In recent years, silicon carbide has also found increasing use in the semiconductor industry.

Another intriguing group of synthetic silicon compounds are the *silicones*. Silicones are organic compounds that contain groupings of silicon and oxygen atoms ($-Si-O-$). First prepared by the English chemist F. S. Kipping in 1899, the silicones now include hundreds of compounds that exist as liquids or solids. They tend to be chemically inert; stable at very high and very low temperatures; resistant to water, ultraviolet radiation, and weather; and nonsticking. Many of the silicones have other properties of special importance in industry.

Because of these properties, silicones have been used widely as lubricants, heat-transfer agents, synthetic rubber, adhesives for electrical and nonelectrical purposes, paint and enamel additives, and electrical insulation. One type of silicone has sold commercially as "Silly Putty."

Other forms of silicone were used extensively during the period from the 1960s to the 1990s as prostheses (for example, for breast enhancement) because they were regarded as inert to body tissues and body fluids. Evidence to the contrary became generally available in the early 1990s, and the use of silicone for such purposes began to decline.

The most important single application of silicon today is probably in the electronics industry. Silicon is a *semiconductor*, that is, a material that conducts an electric current, but not nearly as efficiently as conductors like silver, copper, or aluminum.

In 1947, scientists at the Bell Telephone Laboratories in New Jersey invented a device for using semiconductors to amplify and control the electric current in a circuit, a device known as a *transistor*. Transistors have revolutionized nearly every aspect of electronics today. They are the basis of very small electronic circuits used in compact disc players, portable radios and televisions, video recorders, videocassette recorders (VCRs), and, of course, computers.

The development of semiconductor technology over the past 50 years has created a new and growing market for silicon and its compounds. In response to the needs of this technology, techniques for producing an ultrapure form of silicon had to be developed. Indeed, silicon containing less than 10^{-10} parts of impurities is now routinely produced on an industrial scale, making the substance one of the purest materials commercially available.

Yet another use of silicon (as silicon dioxide) is in optical fibers. An optical fiber is a glass thread that conducts light in much the same way that a copper wire conducts electricity. When a beam of light enters one end of an optical fiber, it travels through the fiber until it emerges at the opposite end. Since a beam of light can carry information just as an electric current can, optical fibers are a potentially important component of communication systems of the future.

The technical problem in using optical fibers in communication systems is to remove as many impurities as possible from the glass. Impurities such as iron(II) ions (Fe^{2+}) absorb light, causing information to become lost within the fiber. Since fibers often have to be many miles long, signal losses of this kind have to be kept to a minimum.

Scientists have now learned how to produce ultrapure glass with impurities of less than one part in a billion. Fiber systems made from this glass have been used to carry 300,000 separate messages at the same time over distances of 60 miles (100 km).

For a period of time, the primary use of germanium has also been in the semiconductor industry. With the development of new materials, the demand for germanium is decreasing somewhat. Because of its ability to transmit light in the infrared region, however, its use in the manufacture of specialized optical glasses is increasing. A small amount of germanium is also used in dental alloys and in superconducting materials.

Relatively small amounts of tellurium are produced and, of that, more than 90 percent is used in making alloys. For example, its addition to stainless steel improves the machinability of the steel. Tellurium oxide (TeO_2) finds limited application as a coloring agent in glass, porcelain, enamel, and ceramics.

Epilogue

The story of the chemical elements is an unending tale. There are no gaps remaining within the periodic table, but chemists continue to search for new elements at the end of the table. Reports of elements 104 through 109 have already been published, but their discoveries have not yet been officially confirmed. In 1982, for example, a research team at the Heavy Ion Research Laboratory in Darmstadt, Germany, announced that they had produced a single nucleus of element 109. Such discoveries continually push forward the borders of our knowledge of the chemical elements although it will be a long time before we can expect to know very much about these superheavy elements.

Chemists also continue to find new uses for the elements and to invent new compounds with new applications. The development of dozens of new compounds to deal with the terrible human immunodeficiency virus (HIV) epidemic is only one example of the way chemists respond to social needs in their research. If you come across a revised version of this book 10 years from now, expect to be amazed by the number of new substances and new uses for the chemical elements it lists. This field is one that never grows old and boring, but is always fascinating for the curious student of chemistry of every age.

Glossary

Actinides: A family of chemical elements that includes element numbers 90 through 103

Alchemy: A prescientific form of natural philosophy that preceded the birth of science and flourished during the Middle Ages

Alkali metals: The elements that make up Group 1 (I) in the periodic table

Alkaline earth metals: The elements that make up Group 2 (IIA) in the periodic table

Allotropes: Two or more forms of an element with significantly different physical and chemical properties

Alloy: A solid or liquid mixture of two or more elements, one of which is a metal

Alpha particle: A helium nucleus, released during some forms of radioactive decay

Amorphous: Lacking in crystalline form

Atmosphere: The gaseous envelope that surrounds the earth

Atom: The smallest part of a chemical element that retains all the properties of that element

Atomic number: The number of protons present in the nucleus of an atom of an element

Atomic weight: The mass of one atom of an element compared to the mass of a single atom of carbon-12

Beta particle: An electron, released during some forms of radioactive decay

Catalyst: A substance that changes the rate of a chemical reaction without undergoing any change itself

Ceramic: A material fashioned out of clay or some other natural earth at room temperature that is then hardened permanently by heating

Compound, chemical: A substance with definite and constant composition, formed when two or more elements combine with one another chemically

Crystalline: Any form of a substance in which atoms and/or groups of atoms have an orderly arrangement

Electrolysis: A process that occurs when an electrical current is passed through a substance

Electron: An elementary particle found in every atom carrying a single negative charge and having a mass about 1/1,800 that of a proton

Element: Any substance that cannot be broken down into a simpler substance by ordinary chemical or physical means

Family, chemical: A group of elements in the same column in the periodic table, all having similar chemical and physical properties

Fission, nuclear: A process by which a large nucleus is broken apart into two roughly equal halves

Formula, chemical: A combination of chemical symbols that show the kinds of elements present in a compound and the proportion of each

Genetic engineering: Any process by which the chemical structure of a deoxyribonucleic acid (DNA) molecule is changed.

Half-life: The time it takes for one-half of a radioactive material to decay

Halogens: The elements that make up column 17 (VIIA) in the periodic table

Hydrosphere: The portion of the planet made up of water (oceans, lakes, rivers, streams, etc.)

Inert: Having little or no tendency to react with other substances

Inorganic: In general, any chemical compound that does not contain the element carbon (carbon oxides and carbonates are some exceptions)

Ionization energy: The energy required to remove a single electron from an atom

Isotopes: Two or more forms of an element whose atoms contain the same number of protons in their nuclei, but which contain different numbers of neutrons; isotopes have the same atomic number, but different atomic weights

Isotope, radioactive: Any isotope that gives off some form of radiation, such as alpha, beta, or gamma radiation

Lanthanides: A group of chemical elements that includes elements 58 through 71 in the periodic table

Lithosphere: That portion of the earth that consists of rocks and other solid material; the term is sometimes used to refer only to the earth's outer crust

Molecule: A combination of atoms joined to each other chemically that behaves as a single unit

Native: Uncombined

Neutron: A subatomic particle found in all atoms, except that of protium, carrying no negative charge and having a mass about equal to that of the proton

Nucleus: The central core of the atom, consisting of protons and neutrons (with the exception of the protium atom)

Organic: Any compound that contains the element carbon (with the exception of the carbon oxides, carbonates, cyanides, and a few other carbon compounds)

Periodic law: A generalization that states that the properties of the chemical elements are periodic functions of their atomic numbers

Phlogiston theory: An explanation for the process of burning first suggested by Johann Becher and Georg Stahl in the late seventeenth century and disproved by Lavoisier in the 1770s

Polymer: Any substance consisting of large, complex molecules formed by the repeated combinations of one or a few small molecules (monomers)

Proton: A subatomic particle carrying a single positive charge that occurs in the atoms of every element

Reaction, chemical: A change in which one or more substances are converted into one or more new substances

Recombinant DNA research: Research in which DNA from two different sources is combined to produce a new form of nucleic acid

Row: A horizontal group of elements in the periodic table

Semiconductor: A substance that conducts electrical current poorly; a better conductor than an insulator, but not nearly as good as a conductor

Sublimation: The process by which a substance changes from a gas to a vapor without first passing through the liquid state

Symbol: A letter or pair of letters used to represent a chemical element

Transistor: A small electronic device that makes use of semiconductors to amplify or control the flow of electrons in a circuit

Transition elements: Those elements found in the center of the periodic table, making up the "B" elements in the American system of labeling the table

For Further Reading

The first place to look for additional information on the chemical elements is any textbook on high school or college chemistry. At one time, such books were, more than anything, a review of the chemical and physical properties, occurrence, preparation, and uses of the elements and their compounds. That approach to the study of chemistry is known as *descriptive chemistry*. Over the past fifty years, textbooks have gotten away from this approach to chemistry and concentrated more on chemical theory. Some modern texts that still contain some descriptive chemistry include the following:

Campbell, J. Arthur. *Chemistry: The Unending Frontier.* Santa Monica, Calif.: Goodyear, 1978.

Greenwood, N. N. and Earnshaw, A. *Chemistry of the Elements.* Oxford: Pergamon, 1990.

Joesten, Melvin D., Johnston, David O., Netterville, John T., and Wood , James L. *World of Chemistry.* Philadelphia: Saunders, 1991.

Manahan, Stanley E. *General Applied Chemistry.* Boston: Willard Grant, 1978.

McQuarrie, Donald A. and Rock, Peter A. *Descriptive Chemistry.* New York: W. H. Freeman, 1985.

Selinger, Ben. *Chemistry in the Marketplace.* Sydney: Harcourt Brace Jovanovich, 1988.

Stine, William R. *Chemistry for the Consumer.* Boston: Allyn and Bacon, 1978.

Wilbraham, Antony C.; Staley, Dennis D.; Simpson, Candace J.; and Matta, Michael S. *Chemistry.* Menlo Park, Calif.: Addison-Wesley, 1990.

If you can find some older textbooks on chemistry, they are likely to include more descriptive chemistry. Of course, such books will be outdated in some ways, although the descriptive chemistry is likely to be of interest. Among the best of the older books are any edition of *Modern Chemistry* (original author Charles E. Dull, published by Henry Holt) and *Chemistry and You* (Bradbury, McGill, Smith, and Baker, originally published by Lyons & Carnahan).

The standard reference on the discovery of the elements is a book by Mary Elvira Weeks and Henry M. Leicester, *Discovery of the Elements* (published by *Journal of Chemical Education*, 7th edition, 1968). Another interesting resource on this topic is D. N. Trifinov and V. D. Trifinov, *Chemical Elements: How They Were Discovered* (New York: State Mutual Books, 1985).

A number of reference books contain a great deal of very specific information about the chemical elements. Among the best of these are the following:

Budavari, Susan, ed. *The Merck Index.* Rahway, N.J.: Merck & Company, 1989.

Hawley, Gessner G., ed. *The Condensed Chemical Dictionary*, 9th edition. New York: Van Nostrand Reinhold, 1977.

Ruben, Samuel. *Handbook of the Elements.* Indianapolis: H. W. Sams, 1967.

Sidgwick, Nevil Vincent. *The Chemical Elements and Their Compounds*, 2 vols. Oxford: Clarendon Press, 1950. A very large work that contains an enormous amount of specific information about the elements.

Weast, Robert C., ed. *CRC Handbook of Chemistry and Physics*, 71st edition. Boca Raton, Fla.: CRC Press, 1970.

Some general books that contain at least a little information on some aspects of the elements include the following:

Asimov, Isaac. *The Search for the Elements.* New York: Basic Books, 1962. An older book, with a limited amount of information on specific elements.

Berger, Sue. *Element of the Week.* Batavia, Ill.: Flinn Scientific, 1989.

Cox, P. A. *The Elements: Their Origin, Abundance, and Distribution.* Oxford: Oxford University Press, 1989.

Emsley, John. *The Elements.* Oxford: Oxford University Press, 1989.

Seaborg, Glenn T. and Valens, Evans G. *Elements of the Universe.* New York: Dutton, 1958. Another older book that deals very nicely with the early history of the actinides.

Index